AMERICA the BEAUTIFUL
LOUISIANA

By Deborah Kent

Consultants

Joe Gray Taylor, Ph.D., Dean, College of Liberal Arts, McNeese State University

William J. Miller, Ed.D., Section Chief, Social Studies, Louisiana State Department of Education

Sue Eakin, Ph.D., Professor of History, Louisiana State University at Alexandria

Claude Oubre, Ph.D., Supervisor of Instruction, St. Landry Parish School Board

Phil Cook, Ph.D., Associate Professor of History, Louisiana Tech University

Robert L. Hillerich, Ph.D., Bowling Green State University, Bowling Green, Ohio

CHILDRENS PRESS®
CHICAGO

The Natchitoches Historic District along the Cane River

Project Editor: Joan Downing
Assistant Editor: Shari Joffe
Design Director: Margrit Fiddle
Typesetting: Graphic Connections, Inc.
Engraving: Liberty Photoengraving

Childrens Press®, Chicago
Copyright © 1988 by Regensteiner Publishing Enterprises, Inc.
All rights reserved. Published simultaneously in Canada.
Printed in the United States of America.
    4 5 6 7 8 9 10 R 97 96 95 94 93 92 91

Library of Congress Cataloging-in-Publication Data

Kent, Deborah.
  America the beautiful, Louisiana.

  (America the beautiful state books)
  Includes index.
  Summary: Introduces the geography, history,
government, economy, industry, culture, historic sites,
and famous people of this Southern state.
   1. Louisiana—Juvenile literature. [1. Louisiana]
I. Title. II. Series.
F369.3.K46 1988   976.3   87-9403
ISBN 0-516-00464-6

Mardi Gras celebration in New Orleans

TABLE OF CONTENTS

Chapter 1
BORN OF THE RIVER

Chapter 2

THE LAND

THE LAND

Curtains of Spanish moss shroud groves of cypress and live oak, and rivers flow *above* the surrounding land. From the pine hills in the north to the wetlands along the Gulf of Mexico, Louisiana is rich with surprise and paradox. Today, as it has been throughout the state's history, the land is Louisiana's greatest resource.

GEOGRAPHY AND TOPOGRAPHY

Louisiana is shaped roughly like a heavy work boot, its frayed toe unraveling into the Gulf of Mexico. The Sabine River forms a portion of the border with Texas to the west, while the Mississippi and Pearl rivers comprise much of the border with the state of Mississippi to the east. Arkansas lies to the north, and to the south, the state faces the Gulf of Mexico.

With an area of 47,752 square miles (123,682 square kilometers), Louisiana is somewhat larger than the state of New York. It ranks thirty-first in size among the states. However, the actual area changes constantly due to land erosion along the coast.

Louisiana is a state of lowlands. Its highest point, Driskill Mountain in the north-central part of the state, stands at only 535 feet (163 meters) above sea level. New Orleans, the lowest point in the state, actually lies 5 feet (1.5 meters) below sea level. Louisiana's land, especially that along the state's many rivers, is very fertile, and excellent for raising crops. But the low, flat land is also subject to devastating floods.

Silt deposited by the Mississippi River as it nears the Gulf of Mexico has formed the great Mississippi Delta.

OLD MAN RIVER

Old Man River,
That Old Man River,
He don't say nothin',
He must know somethin',
But Old Man River,
He just keeps rollin' along.

In this song from the musical *Show Boat*, composer George Gershwin captures the essence of the mighty Mississippi: the slow, silent power of its rolling waters.

From its source in northern Minnesota, the Mississippi River winds its way southward. On its journey through the Midwest, it gathers thousands of tons of rich topsoil, to be deposited little by little as the river nears the Gulf of Mexico. Most of southern Louisiana was created by this gradual accumulation of silt. Each year, the sprawling delta where the Mississippi empties into the Gulf grows by another 1,000 acres (405 hectares).

Above: A levee in Destrehan
Right: A cypress swamp in
southeastern "bayou country"

As it rolls across the low-lying plains of southeastern Louisiana, the Mississippi River is actually higher than the surrounding land. Silt deposits have slowly raised the riverbed and formed bluffs along the banks on either side. Beyond the bluffs, or "frontland," the land slopes away until it is lower than the river itself. Both the frontland and the lower "backland" are superb for farming.

Every few years, prolonged rains swell the Mississippi and threaten to inundate nearby cities, towns, and farms. In an effort to control the river, Louisianians have constructed a vast system of thick earthen walls, or levees, along its banks. Despite these precautions, however, disastrous floods sometimes occur. If a levee breaks, floodwater rushes away from the river, sweeping along everything in its path.

RIVERS, LAKES, AND BAYOUS

Louisiana has 3,400 square miles (8,806 square kilometers) of inland waters. The Red River, the second-most important river in the state, is a tributary of the Mississippi River. Like the Mississippi, the Red River is contained between levees for much of its length. The Atchafalaya River is a distributary, breaking away from the junction of the Mississippi and the Red to flow into the Gulf of Mexico. Some experts predict that during the next major flood, the Mississippi will change course and shift to the bed of the Atchafalaya. Other important rivers include the Calcasieu, Ouachita, Sabine, Tensas, Pearl, and Black.

By far the largest lake in Louisiana is Lake Pontchartrain, located in the southeastern portion of the state. Sprawling over 625 square miles (1,619 square kilometers), Lake Pontchartrain is half the size of Rhode Island. A fisherman anchored in the middle of the lake can imagine himself out at sea, for he cannot glimpse either shore. The water is brackish (part salt water), a combination of fresh water and salt water from the Gulf.

Many other lakes in the Mississippi delta region are also brackish, such as Lake Maurepas and Lake Borgne. Freshwater lakes in Louisiana include Caddo Lake, Lake Bistineau, Black Lake, and Catahoula Lake.

The type of wetland most often associated with Louisiana is the bayou. The term *bayou* is unique to Louisiana, and may be confusing to outsiders. A bayou is generally a small river, but it can be any small, slow-moving inlet or outlet of a lake, river, or the sea. Some bayous contain fresh water. Others are brackish, such as those created where fingers of the Gulf push their way inland. A bayou may branch many times as it wanders through the wetlands along the coast. Most bayous are former mouths of the Mississippi, which has changed course countless times during the past million years. Among Louisiana's chief bayous are the Teche, Lafourche, and Boeuf in the south; and the Dorcheat, Dugdemona, and D'Arbonne in the north.

THE COASTAL WETLANDS

From a low-flying plane, it is sometimes difficult to distinguish Louisiana's coast from the water of the Gulf of Mexico. The shoreline shifts constantly with the rise and ebb of the tide, and it is stippled with pools and marshy ponds. As one writer described it, "This indecisive coastal marsh seems . . . to float like a pad of lilies, anchored in place by the most fragile and tenuous of roots."

Louisiana's coast stretches 397 miles (639 kilometers). But the shore is so ragged with inlets, bays, and islands that the actual coastline measures some 7,721 miles (12,423 kilometers).

Reaching some 20 to 30 miles (32 to 48 kilometers) inland and extending along the coast is a belt of swamps and marshes. Crisscrossed with bayous and dotted with lakes and ponds, these wetlands provide extensive drainage. Until the levees were built, they played a vital role in flood control, absorbing overflow from the Mississippi and other rivers.

The swamps and marshes are a tangled wilderness of sedge grass, rushes, and palmetto scrub. Trailing cloaks of Spanish moss (an air plant related to the pineapple) hang from the branches of cypress and live oaks. The ponds and bayous are alive with bullfrogs, catfish, bass, and crayfish (or crawfish, as they are called in Louisiana). The alligator, once an endangered species, has made a remarkable comeback as a result of careful wildlife management. It is now relatively common and can be hunted legally during a tightly controlled season.

Half the ducks and geese in North America spend the winter along the Louisiana coast. The coastal marshes also provide nesting grounds for the white pelican and the increasingly rare brown pelican, the bird that gives Louisiana its nickname, the Pelican State. The swamps and marshes are home to deer and

Plants and animals that can be found in Louisiana include (clockwise from top left) Spanish moss, white-tailed deer, crawfish, Louisiana herons, nutria, and American alligators.

many other fur-bearing animals, including raccoons, otters, and muskrats. The nutria, a large rodent native to Argentina, was introduced to Louisiana in 1930. Measuring 40 inches (101.6 centimeters) and weighing up to 20 pounds (9 kilograms), the nutria is trapped for its glossy, dark-brown fur.

The wetlands are rich in mineral resources. Here and there in the marshes, huge, underground domes of salt have pushed their way up from deep within the earth. These ''land islands'' also

In the prairie region, fields are sometimes flooded for rice cultivation.

contain major sulfur deposits. Vast reserves of oil and natural gas lie under the wetlands and beneath the waters of the Gulf.

THE PRAIRIE AND THE UPLANDS

Northwest of the wetlands lies a second belt of land known as the Louisiana prairie or Attakapas region. The prairie is dotted with marshes, but much of it is lush grassland that has allowed Louisiana a long-standing cattle-raising tradition. Today much of this region is regularly flooded for rice cultivation.

Nearly half of Louisiana is covered by forest. Farther north, the wetlands and the prairie give way to low, rolling hills thick with pine trees. Timber companies own much of this pine country. Some areas, such as the Kisatchie National Forest, are set aside for recreation and conservation. The uplands also hold major deposits of oil and natural gas.

CLIMATE

Louisiana has a humid, subtropical climate. Winters tend to be mild throughout the state, while summers are uncomfortably hot and sticky. In January, the average temperature in northern Louisiana is 49 degrees Fahrenheit (9 degrees Celsius), compared to 55 degrees Fahrenheit (13 degrees Celsius) in the south. In July, the average statewide temperature is 82 degrees Fahrenheit (28 degrees Celsius).

Louisianians are accustomed to heat waves. Before the advent of air-conditioning, many homes were built in groves of shade trees and were positioned to face a nearby lake or river to catch every breeze. The highest temperature ever recorded in Louisiana was 114 degrees Fahrenheit (46 degrees Celsius) at the town of Plain Dealing on August 10, 1936. But extreme cold is not altogether unknown. On February 13, 1899, the temperature in Minden plummeted to a bone-chilling minus 16 degrees Fahrenheit (minus 27 degrees Celsius).

Rainfall is heavy, especially in summer, and averages about 56 inches (142 centimeters) a year. In contrast, Arkansas receives only 42 inches (106.7 centimeters) annually. New Orleans gets about 62 inches (157.5 centimeters) of rainfall a year—more than any other major American city. Northern Louisiana receives occasional snowfall—about 3 inches (7.6 centimeters) each winter. In the south, however, snow is so rare that one park in New Orleans trucks in tons of it once a year as a special treat for the city's children.

In late summer and early fall, southern Louisiana is sometimes struck by hurricanes that sweep in from the Gulf. One of the worst in recent memory was Hurricane Audrey, which in 1957 killed at least five hundred people in Cameron Parish. (In Louisiana, counties are called parishes). Raging winds toppled telephone poles, uprooted trees, and ripped houses from their foundations. But after every disaster, the stalwart people of Louisiana find a way to rebuild their homes and their lives.

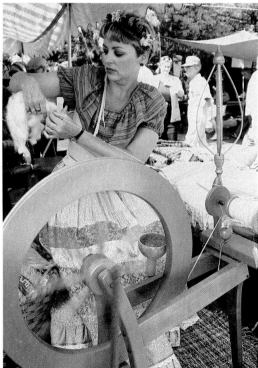

Chapter 3
THE PEOPLE

THE PEOPLE

Every morning at six, Alcide Verret sets off on the bayou in his outboard-powered launch to dredge oysters with a crew of cousins, brothers, and sons. Singing snatches of old songs and bantering in a spicy blend of English and French, they haul in the day's catch. The bayou is Verret's life. He knows every twist and turn, every fishing hole, every hidden path overgrown with bunchgrass.

Many out-of-staters immediately think of someone like Alcide Verret when they picture a typical Louisianian. Actually, bayou fishermen are no more "typical" than the lumbermen of the northern uplands or the people stationed in the Gulf on offshore oil rigs. Louisiana is like a patchwork quilt in which fabrics of many colors and textures are stitched together. Indians and blacks; descendants of early French, Spanish, and English settlers; and immigrants from Ireland, Italy, and Germany are all part of the complex pattern that is Louisiana today.

POPULATION AND POPULATION DISTRIBUTION

Louisiana had 4,206,312 people when the 1980 census was taken—a figure that rose to 4,481,000 according to estimates in 1985. Louisiana ranks nineteenth among the states in population. The state experienced a population boom during the 1960s and

Louisiana's population is made up of people from many different ethnic groups.

1970s, when oil drilling and petroleum-related industries lured job-hungry "immigrants" from all over the country. Between 1970 and 1980, Louisiana's population rose 15.5 percent, compared with a nationwide average growth rate of 11.4 percent. In and around major oil-producing centers such as Lafayette and Morgan City, the population jumped 25 percent. Many of the suburbs around New Orleans saw dramatic population gains as well. However, this trend was sharply reversed in the mid-1980s, when the oil industry went into a decline and jobs became scarce.

New Orleans is Louisiana's largest city, with more than half a million inhabitants. The state's population is heavily concentrated in the oil-refining towns along both banks of the Mississippi between New Orleans and Baton Rouge, the state capital. Other leading population centers surround Shreveport, Monroe, St. Charles, Alexandria, and Natchitoches.

Until the 1940s, Louisiana was primarily an agricultural state. Thirty-one percent of all Louisianians still live on farms or in small towns. Yet every year, more people move to urban centers to seek work and the conveniences of city life. As farming becomes less important, the character of Louisiana is changing.

ETHNIC LOUISIANA

Early in the 1800s, a thirty-eight-year-old black woman known by her African name, Coincoin, was granted her freedom after a lifetime of slavery. In an era when most Louisiana blacks did not own their own lives, and when few women of any race were permitted to act independently, she managed to save enough money to buy the freedom of her children and give them each a parcel of land. Today, many of the people of Isle Brevelle near Natchitoches are the proud descendants of this fiercely determined woman.

Since the colonial era, black people have played a crucial role in Louisiana's history. Today, blacks are the largest single ethnic group in the state, comprising 29 percent of the population. They live in both rural and urban areas throughout the state.

The first white people to establish roots in Louisiana were colonists from France and Quebec. Soon after, they were joined by Spanish traders and adventurers. The descendants of these early French and Spanish settlers were known as Creoles. The term *Creole* originally meant "native of the colony." Over the centuries, its meaning has become blurred by misuse, and today the word means different things to different people.

The early French and Spanish colonists settled in and around New Orleans. To this day, an aura of Old World sophistication is retained by New Orleans, known around the world for its sumptuous dining and elegant homes. In contrast, the character of northern Louisiana resembles that of Arkansas or east Texas. Most

The cosmopolitan character of New Orleans is reflected in its architecture, street names (left), and such annual ethnic festivals as the Festa d'Italia (above).

of the early settlers in the north were cotton farmers from the southeastern states.

People of many other ethnic origins make their homes in Louisiana. A forty-mile (sixty-four-kilometer) stretch of land along the Mississippi River north of New Orleans is still known as the German Coast because of the German farmers who settled there in the early 1720s. The *Isleños* of St. Bernard Parish are the descendants of Spanish Canary Islanders who settled there in the 1770s. Irish and Italian immigrants came to the New Orleans area in the late nineteenth century.

In 1980, more than twelve thousand Louisianians were registered with the Bureau of Indian Affairs as being of Native American descent. The Houma of Pointe d'Ocean in Terrebonne Parish make up the largest group of Native Americans in the state. Although the Houma live chiefly by trapping and fishing, a growing number of them are leaving the bayous and going to the

23

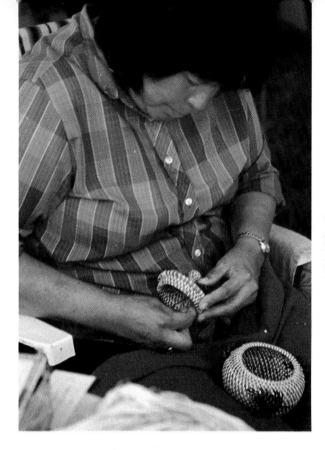

The Coushatta
are one of several
Native American
groups that live
in Louisiana.

cities in search of work. A federal reservation for the Chitimacha
is located near Charenton in St. Mary Parish, and the Coushatta
have reservation land near Elton.

Among the diverse ethnic groups that have come together in
Louisiana, one stands out as especially fascinating. No survey of
the peoples of Louisiana would be complete without a portrait of
the Acadians.

THE ACADIANS

This is the forest primeval. The murmuring pines
  and the hemlocks
Bearded with moss, and in garments green,
  indistinct in the twilight,
Stand like Druids of old, with voices sad and
  prophetic . . .

Lafayette's annual Festival Acadiens celebrates the vibrant culture of the Acadian people.

So begins Henry Wadsworth Longfellow's epic poem *Evangeline*, the moving story of a people called the Acadians. In 1755, British soldiers drove nearly fifteen thousand French colonists from the part of eastern Canada now known as Nova Scotia. The French settlers had named the land Acadia. With only the possessions they could carry on their backs, the refugees set out on a heartbreaking pilgrimage in search of a new home. During the journey, families became separated and thousands died of hunger and disease.

Between 1764 and 1790, about four thousand survivors made their way to Louisiana, where the Spaniards offered to give them land. They settled along Bayou Lafourche and Bayou Teche, along the Mississippi River, near St. Gabriel, and on the southwestern prairies. They lived by farming, hunting, fishing, and trapping.

Today, some half million people of Acadian descent, often known as Cajuns, live in Louisiana. Though many people once felt that the term *Cajun* had negative connotations, it is now

This tiny church on the Blind River can be reached only by boat.

widely accepted. Into the 1950s, some Acadians still learned French as their first language. Today, many Acadian children are being taught French in school in an effort to preserve their language and culture. Some Acadians still live by fishing and trapping, while others own farms, ranches, or find work on Louisiana's oil rigs.

The Acadians are a vibrant, fun-loving people. They are famous for their delicious, spicy food, their lively music, and their dances that shake the rafters from dusk until dawn. They add their share of the zest and color that make Louisiana's culture unique.

RELIGION

A legacy of the original French and Spanish settlers, the Roman Catholic church predominates in southern Louisiana. For most Louisiana Catholics, religion fulfills social as well as spiritual needs. On saint's days and other church holidays, entire towns turn out to eat, drink, and dance. During Mardi Gras season, the people of New Orleans and other southern Louisiana communities party for weeks in preparation for the fasting and sacrifice of Lent.

In religion, as in so many other areas, Louisiana is divided along regional lines. Northern Louisiana is overwhelmingly Protestant. An exception is Natchitoches, which was settled by the French and is still predominantly Catholic. Though virtually every Protestant sect has some followers, the Baptist church and various fundamentalist sects have the largest memberships among both whites and blacks.

POLITICS

Despite the differences between the various regions of Louisiana, the state has been remarkably united in the realm of politics. Before the Civil War, the Republican party took a strong antislavery stand that outraged most white Louisianians—the only Louisianians who could vote. The Democratic party gained Louisiana's overwhelming support and remained unchallenged for over a century. When David Treen was elected governor in 1980, he became the first Republican to hold that office since the 1870s.

In 1981 a reporter asked Louisiana Senator John Breaux, then a congressman, if his vote could be bought. "No," replied Breaux with a mischievous smile, "but it can be rented." No one denies that political corruption has been a deep-seated problem in Louisiana. Yet, the misuse of power receives banner headlines while hundreds of Louisiana officials go quietly about their business, serving honorably and well.

Chapter 4

LOUISIANA BECOMES A COLONY

LOUISIANA BECOMES A COLONY

In the centuries before it became a state, Louisiana knew many masters. The Indians, the French, and the Spanish possessed the land in turn. Each of these peoples played a role in shaping the history and culture of Louisiana.

THE FIRST LOUISIANIANS

One can best perceive the shape of the great mound at Poverty Point from a low-flying plane. A vast earthwork three-fourths of a mile (one kilometer) in diameter, it rises gradually by means of six terraces to a flat platform at the top. Archaeologists think that this mound may have been a foundation for dwellings. The great mound and several other mounds at Poverty Point near Epps are remnants of the earliest-known culture to exist in what is now Louisiana. The people of Poverty Point, who arrived about three thousand years ago, had an advanced society based on agriculture. They traded with other groups as far away as the Ohio Valley.

The Poverty Point civilization vanished by about 700 B.C. Over the next thousand years, many Indian groups rose and fell in Louisiana. Since they left no written records, we know little about them. We know something about the Indians who lived in Louisiana in the 1600s and 1700s, however, through the accounts of early European explorers.

By the early 1600s, several Indian groups lived in Louisiana's swamps, forests, and prairies. In the northeastern corner were the villages of the Tunica. The Muskhogeans lived in the region north of Lake Pontchartrain, and the Caddo could be found in the northwest. The Attakapa and the Chitimacha lived in the south. Each of these main groups was subdivided into several smaller groups, whose languages differed as much from each other as English does from German.

The native people of Louisiana raised corn, pumpkins, squash, melons, and beans. They gathered wild nuts and fruits, hunted game with arrows and blowguns, and set woven nets across streams to catch fish. They decorated their pottery with pictures of birds and animals, and wore beautiful robes of feathers on ceremonial occasions.

Few Europeans had much real sympathy for the Indians. Most, in their relentless search for land and wealth, sought only to exploit them. One Indian group after another was either persuaded to sell its traditional territory or was driven away by force. Actually, the Indians' worst enemy was not European firearms, but the diseases the Europeans brought with them to the New World, such as smallpox, measles, and tuberculosis. The Indians had no immunities against these illnesses, and dreadful epidemics swept through their villages, sometimes wiping out entire populations. Weakened and demoralized, the Indians withdrew ever deeper into the woods and swamps, to live as scattered outcasts in the land that had once been their own.

THE EXPLORERS

For twenty years, the king of Spain had heard rumors of a wondrous river in the New World, its banks lined with villages where people wore so many gold ornaments that they jangled as

Exploring the lower Mississippi River area in 1541, Hernando De Soto and his men may have been the first Europeans to set foot in present-day Louisiana.

they walked. At last, he sent explorer Hernando De Soto to find the fabled river. De Soto trekked overland from present-day Florida, and in 1541 reached the Mississippi River in northwestern Mississippi. Traveling south, his men may have been the first Europeans to set foot in Louisiana. De Soto died, however, before he could descend to the river's mouth.

Since the region did not seem to offer any gold, Spain made little effort to explore the Mississippi any farther. More than a century elapsed before a European expedition finally followed the great river to the Gulf of Mexico.

While studying to become a Jesuit priest, René-Robert Cavelier, Sieur de La Salle, longed for the adventure of faraway places. He begged to go to China as a missionary. When his superiors ordered him to complete his studies first, he abandoned the seminary and left France for the New World. In French Canada, he turned soldier and fortune seeker, and built a series of forts and trading posts along the Great Lakes.

In the spring of 1682, with a small band of Frenchmen and Indians, La Salle set out by canoe down the Mississippi. Their perilous journey brought them at last to the open water of the Gulf of Mexico.

A few miles inland, La Salle led his company ashore for a simple but momentous ceremony. As proof that he came in the name of God, he set up a rough, wooden cross. Then, erecting a pillar adorned with the French coat of arms, he declared that the entire Mississippi River and all of the land drained by its tributaries belonged to the king of France. As prominent American historian Francis Parkman noted, "The vast heartland of the great continent, the entire Mississippi basin, was claimed for the king of France by virtue of a feeble human voice inaudible at half a mile."

The territory claimed by La Salle comprised the central third of the present-day United States—all of the land from the Appalachians to the Rockies, and from the Great Lakes to the Gulf of Mexico. La Salle named this territory after the French king, Louis XIV. He called this immense wilderness empire Louisiana. Part or all of fifteen states would eventually be formed from the region. Only a small part of it would become the state of Louisiana as we know it today.

FRENCH COLONIZATION

King Louis XIV regarded La Salle's gift as a mixed blessing. He had little interest in establishing working colonies in North America, and did not relish the expense of defending his new lands. At the same time, however, he did not want Louisiana to fall into the hands of his archenemies, the British. The British already had a string of colonies along the eastern seaboard, and were eager to acquire even more territory.

In 1698, to discourage further British expansion, the French

Pierre Le Moyne, Sieur d'Iberville (right), founded the French colony
of Louisiana in 1699. Fort St. Jean Baptiste (left), established in
1714 by French trader Louis Juchereau de St. Denis, became the first
permanent European settlement in present-day Louisiana.

king sent explorer Pierre Le Moyne, Sieur d'Iberville, to find the
mouth of the Mississippi from the open sea and found a colony
there. Sailing along the Gulf coast, Iberville reached the river's
mouth on March 3, 1699. The same year, he established a
settlement at Biloxi Bay (near present-day Biloxi, Mississippi) that
became the first capital of the Louisiana colony. Fort de la
Boulaye, built in 1701 on the east bank of the Mississippi some
fifty miles (eighty kilometers) from the Gulf, became the first
European outpost within the boundaries of present-day Louisiana.
More than a decade later, in 1714, Fort St. Jean Baptiste at
Natchitoches on the Red River became Louisiana's first permanent
white settlement.

Few French people were interested in beginning a new life in
the colonies, and Louisiana grew very slowly. At last, in 1717, the
French Crown commissioned the Company of the West to manage
the colony. The Company of the West was run from Paris by a

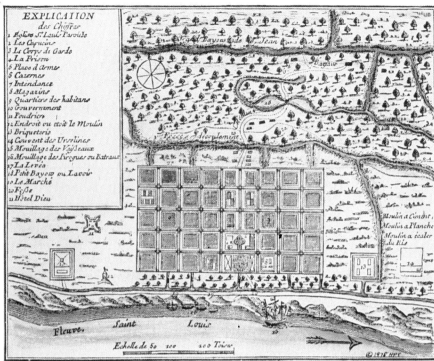

The Company of the West, headed by John Law (left), began managing the Louisiana colony in 1717. Soon after, plans for a new trading post on the Mississippi River (right), to be called New Orleans, were drawn up by the colonial governor, Jean Baptiste Le Moyne, Sieur de Bienville.

smooth-talking professional gambler from Scotland named John Law. Convinced that he could make the colony a lucrative venture, Law persuaded hopeful investors to pour capital into Louisiana.

Law reasoned that the colony would never prosper without more people to work the land. At his urging, the French government offered to release any prisoners who agreed to emigrate to Louisiana. Most convicts, however, preferred prison in France to freedom in the wilderness. Eventually, hundreds of prisoners were sent to the colony against their will. Homeless people were taken from the streets of Paris and other French cities.

Understandably, morale was low among the colonists. They had neither the skill nor the desire to till the soil, and instead resumed

the ways that had put them in prison in the first place. They drank, gambled, and brawled. Their food had to be imported from the West Indies and from farming settlements in Illinois.

The Company of the West was able to recruit some industrious farmers by offering generous land grants to families from Germany. But still more hands were needed. In 1719, Law had a cargo of African slaves brought to the colony. Slavery had been introduced to Louisiana years before, but under the Company of the West it became a crucial part of the economy.

Fired by the dream of a prosperous trading center, the Company of the West asked the colonial governor, Jean Baptiste Le Moyne, Sieur de Bienville (Iberville's brother), to establish a port city on the Mississippi. Bienville selected a spit of land nestled in a curve of the Mississippi River just south of Lake Pontchartrain. In 1718, Adrien de Pauger, a talented engineer, drew the plans for the new town, and the first frame houses were hammered together. Bienville named the town Nouvelle Orleans in honor of the French Duc d'Orleans, the regent of France.

In the beginning, many had doubts about the location of New Orleans, as the port would later be called. Living conditions were dismal. The humid, low-lying country swarmed with mosquitoes that carried deadly malaria and yellow fever. Sanitation was non-existent. There was no sewer system, and when it rained, which was often, the town's unpaved streets turned into a sea of mud. In 1722, a hurricane leveled two-thirds of the town's flimsy houses.

At this point, the settlers might have thrown up their hands and moved to a more hospitable location. But they were determined to carry on, and doggedly, they rebuilt their homes.

Despite John Law's efforts, Louisiana did not prosper. By 1720, it was clear that his scheme to finance the colony had failed, and he fled France in disgrace. The Company of the West, which had been absorbed by the Company of the Indies in 1719, continued to manage the colony. But it was losing money year after year. In 1731, it relinquished its control over the colony, and Louisiana was once again ruled directly by the French Crown.

In 1754, the conflict over American expansion into that part of the Louisiana colony claimed by both England and France erupted into the French and Indian War. Two years later the conflict spread to Europe, where it became known as the bloody Seven Years' War. The war drained France's resources. Louisiana was a liability that the mother country could no longer afford.

SPANISH LOUISIANA

By 1762, it was clear that the French colonies in Canada would fall to the British. But perhaps there was still a way to prevent England from taking over all of the Louisiana territory. On November 11, 1762, by the secret Treaty of Fountainbleau, France voluntarily ceded to Spain New Orleans and the part of the Louisiana colony west of the Mississippi River. Though the Spaniards were reluctant to take on the expense of maintaining this vast holding, they, too, hoped to prevent British expansion. Louisiana would provide a buffer zone between the British colonies and Spain's empire to the west.

On a rainy day in March 1766, the first Spanish governor, Antonio de Ulloa, arrived by ship with eighty soldiers to take

Antonio de Ulloa, Louisiana's first Spanish colonial governor, was driven out in 1768 by French Louisianians who were determined to resist Spanish control over the colony.

charge of the former French colony. A soft-spoken scholar, Ulloa made a poor impression on the French Louisianians. Soon a group of rebels hatched a rumor that he planned to forbid the importation of any wines but those from Spain. To the wine-loving Frenchmen, this was a blow not to be borne. In 1768, Ulloa was denounced and driven from New Orleans.

Spain did not take this uprising lightly. In 1769, the king of Spain sent General Alejandro O'Reilly to re-establish Spanish control in Louisiana. "Bloody O'Reilly," as he was nicknamed by the people of Louisiana, sentenced some of the rebel leaders to be hanged, and made it clear that no further unrest would be tolerated. When he left seven months later, the colony had submitted peacefully to Spanish rule. Within a short time, the French and Spanish reconciled their differences, and even began to intermarry.

With the defeat of the British in the American Revolution, Spain no longer needed Louisiana as a buffer zone. Although Louisiana was prospering under Spanish rule, it still was not economically profitable. In 1800, Napoleon Bonaparte pressured Spain to return the territory to France. Charles IV of Spain agreed, on the condition that France would never cede or sell the territory to any other nation. Within a few short years, Napoleon broke his word, launching Louisiana into the next era of its tumultuous history.

Chapter 5

BECOMING AMERICAN

BECOMING AMERICAN

American President Thomas Jefferson wanted the port city of New Orleans and the Mississippi River system to belong to the young American nation. It was necessary for the development of the country's western frontier. So he sent American statesmen to France to make the purchase. Emperor Napolean was reluctant to sell, but he desperately needed money to finance his European wars. Although negotiations moved slowly, once Napoleon made up his mind, the sale of the Louisiana colony went swiftly and smoothly. Yet long and bitter years would pass before the people of Louisiana would feel they were truly part of the United States.

THE LOUISIANA PURCHASE

The Louisiana Purchase was probably the best real estate bargain in history. For only $15 million, the United States acquired nearly a million square miles (2.6 million square kilometers) of land. The acquisition of this land not only doubled the size of the United States, but also gave it access to the entire Mississippi River system.

Once more, the fate of Louisiana was sealed by a treaty made far away without the consent or even the knowledge of its people. Louisianians had barely gotten used to being "French" again when they discovered, to their dismay, that they were now • "American."

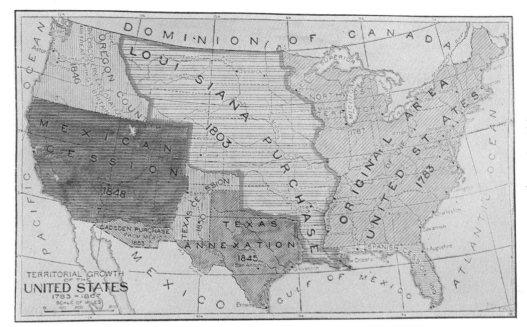

Present-day Louisiana was only a small part of the vast Louisiana Purchase Territory bought by the United States from France in 1803.

The capital of the Louisiana Territory, New Orleans, was a thriving port and the hub of trade along the American frontier. It was also a sophisticated cultural center. There were numerous theaters, and the finest singers of the day performed at the French opera. In the winter, public balls were held twice a week. The Catholic, French-speaking Creoles of New Orleans felt they had nothing in common with the Protestant, English-speaking Americans who intended to govern them. The only Americans they had had contact with were the "Kaintucks," rough-hewn farmers from Kentucky and Tennessee who floated downriver on flatboats and rafts to sell their goods in New Orleans.

Tension mounted when, in 1804, the American government banned the further importation of black slaves to Louisiana. What some Louisianians and other southerners referred to as "that peculiar institution" of slavery was thoroughly entrenched in Louisiana society. Sugar and cotton plantations, on which the entire Louisiana economy was based, required a cheap and dependable source of labor—slaves—to tend and harvest the crops. Many Louisianians grumbled that the Yankees in Washington were trying to bring about their ruin.

In 1804, Congress subdivided the vast Louisiana Territory so that it could be governed more easily. One section, which included all or part of fourteen eventual states, was named the District of Louisiana. The Territory of Orleans became the name for the area that makes up most of modern Louisiana. Two sections of present-day Louisiana were not included in the Territory of Orleans. One was a neutral piece of land along the Sabine River at what is now the western border of the state. The other was a strip of land east of the Mississippi River and north of Lake Pontchartrain. This region, next to the southernmost portions of present-day Mississippi and Alabama, was known as West Florida and was owned by Spain. The people of West Florida, most of whom were of English descent, ousted the Spanish in 1810. West Florida functioned as an independent republic for ten months, and then the western half of it was annexed to the Territory of Orleans.

LOUISIANA BECOMES A STATE

By 1810, the Territory of Orleans had more than seventy thousand people, with about an equal number of blacks and whites. By the provisions of the Northwest Ordinance of 1787, a territory could apply for statehood when it achieved a population of sixty thousand. In 1811, forty-three men gathered in a New Orleans coffeehouse to draw up a state constitution. .

The application for statehood aroused a storm of protest in Congress. Louisiana's culture was more French than American, and many of its people did not speak English. Some questioned whether Louisianians would be loyal to the United States.

Besides, Louisianians had a reputation for lawlessness. Bands of horse thieves and cattle rustlers found refuge in the neutral strip along the Sabine River, which had been established as a buffer zone between Louisiana and Spanish Texas. The notorious pirate Jean Laffite based his gang of plunderers on the islands of Barataria Bay.

Many Louisianians were as reluctant to become American as the Americans were to welcome them. But once the objections were aired, Congress approved the application for statehood. The new state would consist of the original Territory of Orleans and a portion of West Florida extending to the Pearl River. (The neutral section of land along the Sabine River was incorporated nine years later.) On April 30, 1812, Louisiana became the eighteenth state to join the Union.

THE BATTLE OF NEW ORLEANS

In 1812, just as Louisiana was becoming a full-fledged state, America plunged into another war with England. Eventually, the conflict found its way to Louisiana in a battle that has been the subject of legend and song ever since.

In the autumn of 1814, British General Edward Pakenham prepared to attack the vital American port of New Orleans. The American troops in the South were under the command of a fiery Tennesseean named Andrew Jackson, who rallied every available fighting man to defend the city. He reinforced the militiamen with a hundred Choctaws and two battalions of free men of color—blacks who had bought their freedom, been freed by their masters, or had never been slaves. He even enlisted Laffite's pirates, promising them amnesty if they fought for the United States.

On January 8, 1815, General Pakenham launched an all-out

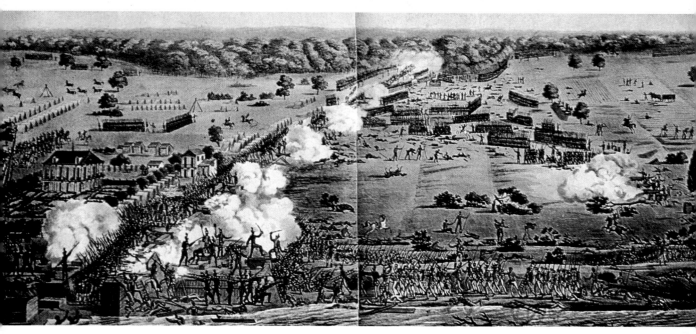

Unaware that a peace treaty had already been signed, British and American troops clashed in the 1815 Battle of New Orleans.

attack at Chalmette, about 6 miles (10 kilometers) from New Orleans. The crossed straps at the front of the British uniforms made a perfect target for the sharp-shooting pirates and frontiersmen. As the British soldiers surged forward, the Americans picked them off one by one. General Pakenham was killed, and when the battle was over, more than two thousand of his men lay dead or wounded. Only seven of Jackson's men died.

The victory gave the people of Louisiana a sense of pride in being American. Andrew Jackson became the state's hero. Thirty years later, New Orleans' Military Plaza was renamed Jackson Square and adorned with a bronze statue of the general astride a rearing horse.

Ironically, the battle should not have taken place at all. A few weeks after Jackson's victory, word reached the United States that the Treaty of Ghent had been signed on December 28, 1814. While hundreds were dying in the Battle of New Orleans, the United States and Great Britain were already at peace.

To honor Andrew Jackson for defeating the British in the Battle of New Orleans, the people of New Orleans adorned the city's Military Plaza, renamed Jackson Square, with a bronze statue of the general.

THE PRICE OF PROSPERITY

No one in Louisiana had seen such a spectacle before. A boat powered not by oars or sails, but by a rumbling engine within its hull. Crowds gathered on the dock to marvel and cheer as the steamboat *New Orleans* chugged and puffed into the port whose name she bore. The *New Orleans'* journey from Pittsburgh opened a fresh chapter in the story of the Mississippi River: the age of the steamboat.

Not only were steamboats faster than the rafts and other boats currently in use—they could travel upriver as well as down. Boats carrying grain and vegetables steamed into New Orleans from the Midwest. Cloth, leather goods, and farm machinery came in from the East Coast by way of the Gulf, to be shipped up to Illinois and Michigan.

By the mid-1800s, New Orleans had become the most important port in the South.

By the early 1800s, Louisiana was producing profitable exports of its own, and by the 1830s, an economic boom was underway. The invention of the cotton gin in 1793 and the discovery in 1795 of a new way to granulate sugar on a large scale paved the way for thriving cotton and sugar industries in Louisiana. The humid climate of southern Louisiana proved ideal for growing sugarcane, while cotton flourished along the rivers in the north.

The cultivation of both crops required many hands. Thousands of black slaves hoed fields, picked cotton, and boiled cane juice. The state's economy depended on their labor.

Most of Louisiana's farmers in the first half of the nineteenth century tilled only a few acres, growing barely enough corn, squash, and turnips to feed their families. But 43 percent of the state's arable land belonged to some sixteen hundred great plantations, each worked by fifty or more slaves. Soon after Louisiana entered the Union, this handful of planters came to dominate the state politically and philosophically.

Although a small number of planters owned splendid plantations (above left), some complete with a guesthouse called a garçonier (above), most nineteenth-century Louisianians were subsistence farmers who owned no slaves and lived on small farms of only a few acres (left).

Each plantation consisted of a "big house" for the master and his family, and a series of smaller outbuildings. These might include a *garçonier* (a house for male visitors and grown, unmarried sons); a kitchen, kept separate to keep away cooking odors and prevent the main house from catching fire; and a *pigeonnier*, as pigeons were used to carry messages between neighboring plantations. The plantation would also have storehouses, stables, and several slave cabins.

Plantation slaves, who were bought and sold as property (right), often lived in cabins such as this one (above), now part of the Rural Life Museum in Baton Rouge.

Only a very small percentage of the rural population, perhaps 1 or 2 percent, were truly wealthy, but these few lived in almost regal splendor. They enjoyed entertaining guests on a grand scale. On such plantations, the big house was equipped with a ballroom where dances were held. The dining-room table might seat as many as thirty guests. The mistress of the house always insisted on the finest silver and china, often purchased in Europe.

Early in the nineteenth century, a movement for the abolition of slavery gathered strength in the northern states. But in Louisiana, as elsewhere in the South, books and pamphlets that sought to justify slavery's existence were distributed. Some writers argued that slavery was condoned by the Bible, and insisted that black people were better off as Christian slaves than as African pagans.

To most planters, slaves were property and nothing more. A healthy adult male sold for at least $800 in the slave market at

New Orleans, and a female sold for somewhat less. Some slaves, especially in New Orleans, became carpenters, blacksmiths, or shopkeepers, and were permitted to keep a share of their profits for themselves. But in general, the slave's life was one of drudgery, with no hope for improvement.

The worst feature of slavery was that a slave had no control over his own fate. If the master had a bad harvest, he might sell some of his slaves to pay his debts. If he died, his estate could be broken up and his property disposed of. Husbands and wives could be parted without warning. In fact, marriages between slaves were not even legally recognized, although there were many permanent unions. Children over the age of ten could be sold away from their mothers, never to see them again. Even today, the phrase "sold down the river" means to be betrayed.

In 1811, a mulatto named Charles Deslonde and a slave called Jupiter organized a large slave rebellion in St. John the Baptist Parish. The rebels were poorly armed, and they were soon captured and executed. But this insurrection, and many similar incidents, instilled a deep fear in the white people of Louisiana. As the antislavery movement in the North grew more vocal, the laws controlling slaves in Louisiana became more and more repressive. It was illegal for anyone to teach a slave to read or write. In 1830, it became a capital crime to make any public statement that might incite rebellion. By 1852, slaves could not be granted their freedom under any circumstances.

While the slaveholding planters were only a small minority of white Louisiana, their power, secured by a network of controls, enabled them to set the tone on the slavery issue throughout the state. In their desperate struggle to preserve "that peculiar institution," they led Louisiana further and further down the road to disaster.

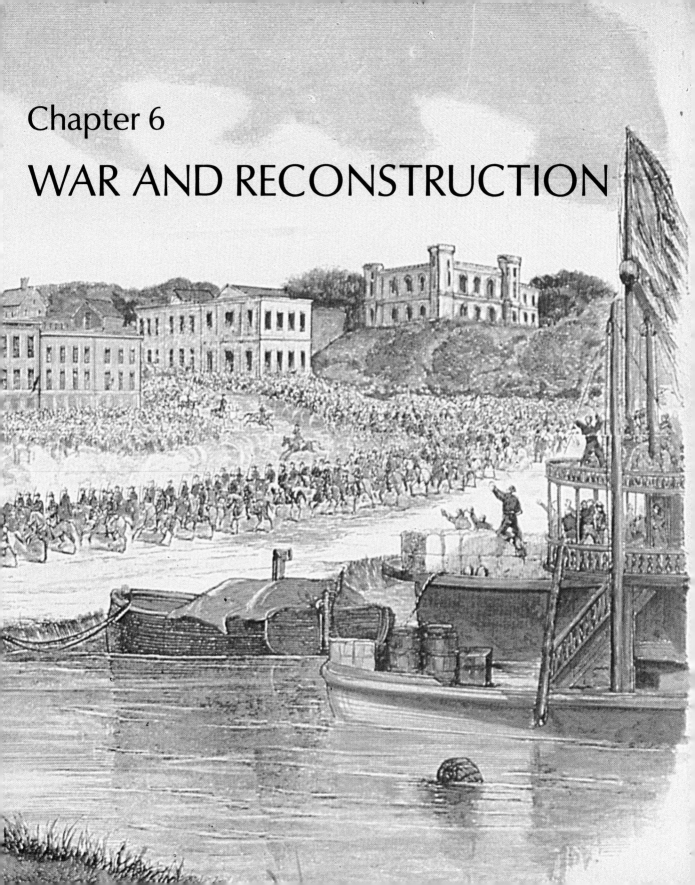

Chapter 6

WAR AND RECONSTRUCTION

WAR AND RECONSTRUCTION

During the presidential campaign of 1860, debate over the slavery question split the nation. The recently organized Republican party stood on a solid antislavery platform. Many Louisiana legislators echoed the sentiments voiced in other southern states, and vowed that Louisiana would secede from the Union if a Republican were elected.

In November, 1860, Republican candidate Abraham Lincoln was elected sixteenth president of the United States. Four months later, on March 21, 1861, Louisiana officially joined the newly formed Confederate States of America.

LOUISIANA IN THE CIVIL WAR

A spirit of holiday excitement swept Louisiana in the spring of 1861. A rash of balls celebrated the new Confederacy. Ladies stitched flags and officials made flowery speeches about the glory of the South.

All over the state, eager young men rushed to enlist in the Confederate army. Spectators cheered and flung flowers as the recruits paraded down dusty, small-town streets. These were the tough, proud men of the South. Why, one Johnny Reb could beat five Yankees single-handed!

By the close of 1861, the reality of war was brought home to Louisiana. Union ships blockaded the mouth of the Mississippi River and most of the ports along the Gulf, cutting off the flow of

In 1862, Union naval troops captured New Orleans after carrying out a fiery attack (above) on the two Mississippi River forts guarding the city.

supplies to Confederate troops and civilians. Early in April 1862, the South suffered a crushing defeat at Shiloh in Tennessee. For two weeks, trains and steamboats carried thousands of wounded and dying men into New Orleans, where they received primitive care in makeshift army hospitals.

Then, late in April, Union Captain David Farragut and a fleet of forty-four ships sailed up the Mississippi from the Gulf to attack New Orleans itself.

New Orleans relied on two forts for its main defense. Fort Jackson and Fort St. Philip faced each other across the river a number of miles below the city. Between the forts stretched a massive iron chain. According to the Confederate strategy, the chain would hold back Farragut's ships and they could then be destroyed by cannonfire from the forts. But Farragut cut the chain by night, and after a fierce battle, swept past the forts to New Orleans.

Union troops feeding hungry people in occupied New Orleans in 1862

On the afternoon of April 24, as some Orleanians fled and others watched in helpless rage, Farragut's fleet reached the city. Poorly armed and demoralized, the people of New Orleans knew that resistance was futile. Confederate General Mansfield Lovell, knowing he could not defend the city, withdrew his troops, and New Orleans became an occupied city.

Farragut continued up the Mississippi to take Baton Rouge, the state capital. He left New Orleans under the command of one of the most despised figures in Louisiana history, General Benjamin F. Butler.

A Massachusetts millionaire, Benjamin Butler hated the South and regarded the citizens of New Orleans as a conquered people. From the first, he stamped out any spark of rebellion. When a professional gambler named William Mumford tore the newly hoisted Stars and Stripes to shreds, Butler had him hanged for

After capturing New Orleans, Union Captain David Farragut (left) left the city under the command of General Benjamin F. Butler (right), one of the most hated figures in Louisiana history.

treason. Mumford became a martyr, but after his death few Orleanians defied Butler's rule.

The women did not submit so easily. They bombarded the Yankee troops with insults, spat at them, and sometimes pelted them with rotten eggs. In retaliation, Butler passed the infamous "Woman Order," stating that any woman who insulted Union soldiers would be treated as a common woman of the streets— arrested, jailed, and fined. The genteel ladies of New Orleans were outraged. They nicknamed the Yankee general "Beast Butler" and put his picture in their chamber pots.

Butler was recalled by the end of 1862, but he left his mark on New Orleans for posterity. On the base of the statue of Andrew Jackson in Jackson Square he inscribed the words, "The Union must and shall be preserved."

RESISTANCE AND DEFEAT

Though Butler was the Union officer most hated by the people of Louisiana, his successor, General Nathaniel P. Banks, did far more damage to the Confederate cause. In late spring of 1863, Banks led forty thousand Union troops, including two regiments

The formal surrender of Port Hudson, the last Confederate stronghold on the Mississippi River

of free men of color and runaway slaves, against the Confederate stronghold of Port Hudson north of Baton Rouge. Port Hudson was well fortified and had enough food and ammunition to withstand a long siege. With only seven thousand men, the Confederate commander, General Franklin Gardner, repulsed three Union assaults. Finally, after six weeks, Gardner's supplies were exhausted. When he received news of the disastrous Confederate defeat at Vicksburg in Mississippi, he raised the white flag of surrender.

The conquests of Vicksburg and Port Hudson gave the Union forces control of the entire Mississippi River and effectively cut the Confederacy in two. In Louisiana, only the northern and western parts of the state remained in rebel hands. The following year, General Banks moved up the Red River to capture Alexandria and Natchitoches. His plan to take the Confederate state capital of Shreveport, however, was eventually frustrated by Confederate General Richard Taylor. In the bloody Battle of Mansfield, Banks and his men met a punishing defeat.

The retreating Union forces nevertheless waged a brutal campaign against the morale of Louisiana's people. On their trek

After New Orleans became occupied, Confederate men who wished to remain in the city had to sign an oath of allegiance to the United States.

through the countryside they slaughtered livestock and seized any food they could find. As often as possible, Louisianians destroyed their own stores of food and cotton to keep them from the Yankees.

The people of Louisiana would have suffered even more had it not been for the heroic efforts of Henry Watkins Allen, who became governor of Confederate-held Louisiana in 1864. Allen opposed the burning of supplies and developed a healthy cotton trade with Mexico. With the proceeds, he created widows' pensions and assisted families whose men were in the army. He bought military provisions, opened an iron foundry in Shreveport, and set up a state-run laboratory to manufacture desperately needed medical supplies.

By the spring of 1865, it was clear that the South could hold out no longer. On April 9, Confederate General Robert E. Lee surrendered at Appomattox Courthouse, Virginia. Two months later, the last Confederate troops surrendered at Shreveport. The war was over at last, but its echoes would resound through Louisiana for generations to come.

THE ERA OF RECONSTRUCTION

The Civil War left Louisiana in ruins. More than eleven thousand of the state's young men had died, and just as many came home with disabling wounds. The returning soldier was likely to find his fields untended, his horses and oxen slaughtered by the Yankees. Never again would life be what it had been before the war.

In 1867, the federal government launched a program of military reconstruction aimed at bringing the defeated South back into the Union. Federal officials arrived in Louisiana to oversee elections. Backed by armed troops, they registered black voters and denied the vote to all whites who had aided the Confederacy. In 1868, a charming, twenty-six-year-old Republican named Henry Clay Warmoth was elected governor. Serving under him as lieutenant governor was Oscar Dunn, a former slave.

The Unionist Republicans who controlled Louisiana during the Reconstruction period claimed that they wanted to insure equal rights for the state's black citizens. But many of them exploited their positions by soliciting bribes, embezzling state funds, and rigging elections in order to stay in power. Such men were known as carpetbaggers. Governor Warmoth and his followers grew richer every year.

Some white Democrats fought to regain political control of Louisiana by forming militant, underground, antiblack and anti-Republican organizations. One of these was the White League, which was made up of ex-Confederate soldiers and prominent native Louisianians. In 1874, hundreds of White League members lynched six white Republicans at Coushatta in northwestern Louisiana. Two weeks later, trouble flared in New Orleans between a White League regiment and the government militia. As

In 1867, with the passage of the federal Military Reconstruction Acts, blacks in New Orleans voted for the first time.

the White League attempted to collect a shipment of arms arriving by steamboat, the militia barred the way to the waterfront. Thousands of spectators looked on from their windows as a pitched battle ensued. In the end, the militia yielded, and the White League claimed victory in the Battle of Liberty Place.

It was clear that the Republicans could not control Louisiana without the help of the United States Army. But the federal government was unwilling to commit itself to further military intervention. In 1877, the last federal troops withdrew, and the Reconstruction era came to a close.

Power reverted to the planters, bankers, and merchants who had controlled the state before the war. They became known as the Bourbons, after an old family of European aristocrats. It was said that they "had learned nothing and forgotten nothing." They promoted fear of blacks, hatred of the North, and love of the Confederacy that might have been. With all of the controls at their command under the revived plantation system, the Bourbons would cling to their power until 1928.

Chapter 7
INTO THE TWENTIETH CENTURY

INTO THE TWENTIETH CENTURY

"We declare emphatically that the interests of the white and colored races in the South are identical. Equal justice and fairness must be accorded to each." This was the stand taken by the radical Populist party in the 1890s. But the struggle toward racial equality and greater opportunity for all citizens, whether black or white, followed Louisiana far into the twentieth century.

THE POWER OF THE BOURBONS

In 1896, the ruling Bourbon Democrats found their control over Louisiana challenged by the newly formed Populist party. The Populists hoped to unite all of the state's non-planters and poor people, both black and white. Their candidate for governor, John N. Pharr, promised he would establish an honest government.

The Bourbons were the masters of every known form of vote fraud. "The Populists and Republicans are our legitimate political prey," they proclaimed in the Shreveport *Evening Judge*. "Rob them? You bet! What are we here for?" The Bourbons took charge of the ballot counting, and Pharr met a crushing defeat. But the experience frightened the Bourbons. Never, they vowed, must such a threat to their power be allowed to rise again.

In 1898, the Bourbon leaders met in Baton Rouge to draw up a new state constitution. Blatantly, without apology, the new laws denied the vote to the state's blacks and to many poor whites.

Now, in order to vote, a man had to either own three-hundred-dollars'-worth of property or be able to read and write. Few blacks owned land, and 70 percent were illiterate. The situation among poor whites was little better. To avoid disenfranchising an overwhelming number of white voters, however, the new constitution contained a "grandfather clause." A man could vote if his father or grandfather had been registered by 1867 — the year before black suffrage had gone into effect.

Between 1898 and 1904, the number of white voters in Louisiana dropped by nearly half. The new constitution had an even more devastating effect on blacks. In 1897, 130,000 blacks were registered to vote. By 1904, that number had plunged to 1,342.

In the 1890s, white leaders had enacted a series of "Jim Crow" laws enforcing the time-honored southern custom of keeping the races separate. Blacks and whites had to ride in separate railway cars, eat in separate restaurants, use separate drinking fountains, and attend separate schools. The accommodations for blacks were almost always inferior to those for whites.

As in most other southern states, blacks accused of crimes in Louisiana seldom received a fair trial. White judges and all-white juries ruled against them and exacted harsh penalties. Sometimes there was no trial at all, and the accused was simply lynched — captured and executed by a mob.

Few rural blacks could afford to buy land, and after the Civil War, most worked as sharecroppers for planters. Thousands of whites driven from their small farms by the crumbling post-war economy fared little better. By the turn of the century, black and white sharecroppers were providing most of the labor on large farms and plantations throughout Louisiana.

On the surface, the sharecropping system sounds fair enough.

Southern sharecroppers bringing a bale of cotton to market in 1910

The planter, or landlord, would share the year's harvest with the families who worked his land. But throughout the long year before the cotton or cane went to market, the sharecroppers had to buy food and clothing. Usually, the landlord ran a small general store, called a commissary, where the sharecropper could purchase goods on credit. As soon as he received his earnings for the year, the sharecropper had to pay back his loan, generally at an exorbitant rate of interest. There was rarely anything left over to carry him into the year ahead, and the cycle of borrowing began once more. Unlike slaves, sharecroppers could not be bought or sold. But poverty and debt bound them to the land they farmed.

Not all white Louisianians condoned injustice and poverty. In 1904, Governor Newton Blanchard shocked the legislature when he stated, "The Negro is here. He is a man and a citizen." Blanchard spoke out against lynching, and channeled more funds

An early photograph of Louisiana's first commercial oil field, which came in near Jennings in 1901

into both black and white schools. Even so, for the poor people of Louisiana, social change was agonizingly slow.

GIFTS FROM THE LAND

Louisianians had long prized cypress wood as a material for furniture and houses that withstood the humid climate and the ravages of insects. In the 1880s, the Yankee-run timber industry began to exploit the cypress stands in the southern wetlands on a grand scale. With no thought to conservation, northern lumbermen demolished these forests of great, gnarled trees. By 1900, the timber stands in the swamps were depleted, and the lumbermen turned their attention to the pine woods of the northern uplands. Trees tumbled and sawmills whirred until the pinelands, too, had nothing more to give.

Lured by cheap land, farmers from Germany and the Midwest emigrated to Louisiana in the 1880s to become rice growers on the

Attakapas prairie. By the turn of the century, Louisiana was one of the leading producers of rice in the nation, a position it still holds today. Timber and rice did much to bolster the state's economy. But locked deep beneath the surface of the earth lay the greatest treasure of all.

"We heard a noise and saw the oil go out. At first we thought it was black smoke from the boiler at the well. But it kept on blowing, and we saw the mud blow out over the derrick." Years later, a farmer named Louis Clement recalled the thrill of that day in 1901 when Louisiana's first oil well came in on his land near the town of Jennings. Within a year, seventy-six companies were extracting oil from a huge reserve hidden beneath Louisiana's soil. In 1909, the opening of an oil refinery in Baton Rouge launched Louisiana's petrochemical industry. Over the years, refineries and factories sprouted along the Mississippi from Baton Rouge to New Orleans.

Oil was not the only mineral resource in Louisiana. Sulfur mines opened in Calcasieu and Plaquemines parishes, and Avery Island supported a profitable saltworks. Commercial drilling for natural gas began near Monroe in 1916, and then expanded to most other parts of the state.

By the 1920s, hundreds of corporations were fattening on Louisiana's mineral resources. Yet on the farms, mule teams were more common than tractors. Louisiana had fewer than 300 miles (483 kilometers) of paved roads. Not one bridge spanned the Mississippi River on its 600-mile (965-kilometer) course through the state. Many schools were open for only a few months each year, and some rural areas had no schools at all.

The people of Louisiana were ready for a change. That change came in the form of an ambitious young lawyer named Huey Pierce Long.

THE ERA OF HUEY LONG

The eighth of nine children, Huey Long was born in Winn Parish in 1893. Winn Parish was a stronghold of the Populist movement in the 1890s, and Socialist sentiments were strong in the area during the years before World War I. As a boy, Long absorbed many of the ideas that came out of this Populist-Socialist tradition. Eventually, as a politician, he would use these ideas to defeat the planters who had controlled the state since the days of the earliest European settlements.

After an argument with one of his teachers, Long dropped out of high school and went to work as a traveling salesman. As he peddled cooking oil from house to house, he developed remarkable powers of persuasion. He eventually took law courses at Tulane University, passed the state bar exam, and opened a practice in Winnfield, but his passion was politics. In 1918, at the age of twenty-five, he won the office of railroad commissioner of northern Louisiana, thus launching what was to be a flamboyant political career.

Long's strong anti-corporation stand as a railroad commissioner earned him a devoted following. In 1924 he ran for governor, and although he was defeated in that race, he ran again four years later. He campaigned all over the state, promising better roads and free textbooks. He pledged to help poor farmers, support labor unions, and curtail the power of the corporations. The voters gave Long a chance to fulfill his promises, electing him governor of Louisiana in 1928.

As governor, Huey Long fulfilled many of his campaign promises. He increased funding for education, and provided free textbooks for all schoolchildren. He began construction of bridges at Baton Rouge and New Orleans, improved New Orleans'

Huey P. Long, shown here in a typical speaking pose, was the most powerful politician in Louisiana history.

Charity Hospital, and paved hundreds of miles of roads throughout the state. But Long could be ruthless toward anyone who opposed him. His gleaming new State Capitol Building, towering thirty-four stories above the streets of Baton Rouge, was a monument to his lust for power.

In 1930, as America sank into the most severe economic depression in its history, Huey Long won a seat in the United States Senate. In Washington, he advocated a "share-the-wealth" program that sought to redistribute the vast fortunes of the rich. His popularity swelled among the nation's poor people, and he was clearly gathering momentum for a presidential race in 1936.

As his ambitions soared, Long worked harder than ever to maintain his base of power at home. One night in September 1935, he called a special meeting of the state legislature. Among the many items on the agenda was a bill to gerrymander (rearrange the boundaries of) the district of one of Long's political enemies, Judge Benjamin Pavy.

No one is certain exactly what happened on that fateful night. Walking down the corridor of the Capitol Building, Long is thought to have greeted Pavy's son-in-law, Dr. Carl Weiss. Then, witnesses claimed, Weiss shot Long in the abdomen at point-blank range. Instantly, Long's bodyguards flew into action, pelting Weiss with a deadly volley of bullets. But Long had been fatally wounded. As he lay on his deathbed, he is said to have pleaded, "God, don't let me die! I have so much to do!"

CHANGES AND CHALLENGES

Long's death left the state with a legacy of officials who used every form of corruption to line their pockets. One scandal after another emerged in an epoch journalists nicknamed "The Louisiana Hayride." Yet Long did much to improve life for the state's poor people. Moreover, he broke the hold of the old Bourbon power elite, thus paving the way for greater change in the years ahead.

During the Great Depression, the majority of Louisianians lived below the poverty level. More than 15 percent of the population went on relief, a rate exceeded in only four other states. Many unemployed young men found jobs through the federally sponsored Civilian Conservation Corps (CCC), working on soil-conservation and reforestation projects.

Louisiana, like the rest of the nation, finally emerged from the depression when the economy was stimulated by preparation for World War II. One of the state's greatest contributions to the war effort was the Higgins Shipyards in New Orleans, which led the nation in the production of small naval craft. More than a million new recruits underwent basic training at Fort Polk near Leesville.

Between 1940 and 1950, the number of manufacturing jobs in Louisiana doubled. At the same time, farming became far more mechanized, and the old-fashioned sharecropping system gradually disappeared. Many rural people sought jobs in Baton Rouge, Shreveport, and other cities, while thousands more migrated to the northern states. During World War II and in the following years, nearly half of Louisiana's blacks left the state.

In 1954, the United States Supreme Court made a decision with far-reaching implications for Louisiana and all of the South. In the case of *Brown vs. Board of Education of Topeka*, the Court ruled that racial segregation in the schools was unconstitutional. The judges mandated that the integration of public schools throughout the country should "proceed with all deliberate speed."

Slowly, warily, Louisiana took its first steps toward the integration of some public facilities. Integration of some of the state's universities, including Southwestern, Southeastern, and McNeese, began in the mid-1950s. In 1958, New Orleans abolished segregation on city buses. But on the issue of integration in the public schools, the state legislature refused to budge. Finally, in 1960, the Orleans Parish School Board yielded to pressure from a federal judge and agreed to allow integration of first-grade classes at two of New Orleans' public schools.

On November 14, a six-year-old black girl named Ruby, dressed in her Sunday best, kissed her mother good-bye at the front door of the William Frantz School in New Orleans. She was one of four black children to enroll in two previously all-white schools on that historic morning. Most white pupils stayed home, and the following day their parents organized a massive rally. The segregationist spokesman Judge Leander Perez delivered an inflammatory speech on the evils of integrated education.

The mounting hysteria ultimately resulted in two days of rioting. No one died, but dozens of people were shot, stabbed, and beaten. Some 250 people were arrested, and the city finally lapsed into a sullen truce.

The riots made headlines all over the country. Dismayed by the adverse publicity, 160 New Orleans businessmen banded together and persuaded the community to accept integration, at least on a token basis. The city elected a new mayor, Victor Schiro, who announced he would tolerate no disorder of any kind. In 1961, several New Orleans schools were peacefully integrated. Ten years later, some two hundred thousand Louisiana children were attending integrated schools.

The passage of the Federal Voting Rights Act of 1965 forced Louisiana to end its restrictions against black voters. The last of the state's Jim Crow laws was officially abolished in 1972. In 1978, a black man named Ernest "Dutch" Morial was elected mayor of New Orleans—less than twenty years after Ruby set foot in the William Frantz school for the first time.

In 1972, Edwin Edwards became the first Acadian since 1853 to be elected governor of Louisiana. Through the 1970s and 1980s, Edwards dominated the state's political scene. A notorious gambler, he once revealed that he kept $800,000 in ready cash in case he should suddenly decide to fly to Las Vegas. In 1985 Edwards was indicted on federal racketeering charges, but after twenty months he was finally acquitted.

Louisiana made tremendous gains in the 1970s. New roads and highways began to crisscross the state, giving once-isolated rural

After some initial resistance, integration of Louisiana's schools proceeded smoothly in the 1960s and 1970s.

people access to bustling urban centers. The state's education budget rose, while the illiteracy rate plummeted. College enrollment doubled, and per-capita income climbed.

Then, in 1983, without warning, prices on the world oil market slumped. Louisiana's economy, built on the petroleum industry, sagged on the verge of collapse. By 1986, unemployment in Louisiana had reached 13 percent, higher than any other state.

Yet even in this crisis, the distinctive features of its land and its unique blend of cultures continue to make Louisiana a fascinating and distinctive place to live.

71

Chapter 8

GOVERNMENT AND THE ECONOMY

GOVERNMENT AND THE ECONOMY

GOVERNMENT

Modeled on the federal government, the government of Louisiana consists of three main branches. The legislative branch is concerned with making and repealing laws. The judicial branch, or court system, interprets these laws. The executive branch, or office of the governor, is responsible for enforcing or carrying out the laws.

Like the United States Congress, Louisiana's legislature has an upper house, or senate, and a lower house, or house of representatives. Louisianians elect 39 state senators and 105 representatives to speak for them in the legislature.

The judicial branch consists of the state supreme court, four courts of appeals, and thirty-two lower district courts scattered throughout the state. When Louisiana entered the Union in 1812, it brought along a remnant of its French heritage—a system of civil law based on the Napoleonic code of France. Every other state in the nation follows the English common-law system, whereby judges base their rulings on previous court decisions. Judges practicing under the Napoleonic Code rely heavily on a body of written laws, and are not bound by the decisions of judges in earlier cases.

The governor of Louisiana may be elected an unlimited number of times, but he may serve only two consecutive terms. The governor may veto any bill passed by the legislature. His veto can be overturned by a two-thirds vote in both houses, though this has never happened in the twentieth century. The governor appoints heads of government departments, but must have senate approval.

Louisiana is divided into sixty-four units of local government called parishes. This term is a legacy from the days of French and Spanish rule, when a parish was a district administered by the Catholic Church. Today most parishes are governed by a body called the police jury.

About one-fourth of Louisiana's revenue comes from federal grants and programs. The remainder is raised through state taxes. Personal income tax has risen in recent decades, but it is still relatively low. The state has no property tax. In the late 1980s, a crippled state economy brought on by the slump in the oil industry resulted in a lack of state funds. The state government was unable to expand, or even, in some cases, sustain many of its services. Some state parks had to be closed, and public schools were in desperate need of funds.

EDUCATION

Public education in Louisiana progressed slowly because of weak support in the state legislature. Not until 1916 did Louisiana law require all children between the ages of six and sixteen to attend school. Louisiana still has one of the highest illiteracy rates in the nation, but today the state is striving to make education one of its leading priorities.

Some of Louisiana's schools of higher education have earned outstanding reputations. Tulane University in New Orleans is noted for its graduate programs in law, medicine, and chemistry.

Barge traffic on
the Mississippi River
near the port city
of New Orleans

The main branch of Louisiana State University is located in Baton
Rouge, and smaller branches have sprung up in Shreveport, New
Orleans, Alexandria, and Eunice. Another important school is
Louisiana Tech University in Ruston. Other state-supported
colleges are Southern University in Baton Rouge (with branch
campuses at New Orleans and Shreveport), the University of
Southwestern Louisiana in Lafayette, Northeast Louisiana
University in Monroe, Northwestern State University in
Natchitoches, McNeese State University in Lake Charles,
Grambling State University in Grambling, and Southeastern
Louisiana University in Hammond. Grambling State, Dillard, and
Southern universities were founded as colleges for blacks. By the
late 1960s, all of Louisiana's colleges and universities were
integrated.

TRANSPORTATION AND COMMUNICATION

The romantic era of the Mississippi steamboat reached its peak
in the 1880s. But today the Mississippi River carries hundreds of
times more traffic than it did a century ago. Constant dredging of

75

Louisiana is a leading producer of soybeans, sugarcane, cotton (above), and rice (right).

the river has enabled oceangoing ships to sail upriver all the way to Baton Rouge, even though it is 235 miles (378 kilometers) from the Gulf. New Orleans, which serves about five thousand ships each year, handles more tonnage than any other port in the nation.

In 1928, Louisiana had only 331 miles (533 kilometers) of paved roads. By the mid 1980s, 55,000 miles (88,495 kilometers) of roads and highways linked every city and small town in the state. Today freight trains run along 4,000 miles (6,436 kilometers) of track, and the state is served by fifteen airlines. Louisiana has 290 airports. New Orleans International Airport not only provides access to all parts of the United States, but is also a major point of connection to Central and South America.

This vast system of airports, highways, and railroads makes Louisiana accessible to nearly three million tourists each year.

Tourism is big business in Louisiana. It brings in more than $3.5 billion a year to the state's economy.

Twenty-five daily newspapers and eighty-five weeklies operate in Louisiana. Over several generations, four major papers merged to form the *Times-Picayune/States-Item* of New Orleans. Among the state's other important newspapers are Shreveport's *Times* and the *Baton Rouge Advocate*.

Louisiana's first radio stations, WWL in New Orleans and KWKH in Shreveport, began broadcasting in 1922. Today, the state has 170 licensed radio stations and 22 television stations.

AGRICULTURE

According to a popular legend, a wealthy Louisiana sugarcane planter named Valcour Aimé once made a ten-thousand dollar bet with a houseguest that every item he was serving at a sumptuous banquet had been grown on his own plantation. Sure enough, the chickens, the rice, the coffee, and, to the guest's chagrin, even the after-dinner cigars had been produced on his land. Though tobacco was not considered a Louisiana crop, Aimé raised a rare species called perique that was grown only in St. James Parish.

Today, agriculture accounts for only 2 percent of Louisiana's gross state product (GSP), the yearly sum of all earnings from businesses and service providers in the state. Even so, farming in the Pelican State is as diverse as it was in Valcour Aimé's time. Louisiana ranks second among the states in the production of sweet potatoes, rice, and sugarcane. The state is also a leading producer of cotton and strawberries. Citrus orchards thrive along the sunny Gulf coast. Louisiana pecans are an essential ingredient in dozens of delectable recipes for pies and candies, including the famous praline.

After World War II, Louisiana farmers were delighted to find that many new uses were being found for a familiar crop—soybeans. Soybeans required little labor and grew well in most parts of the state. By the mid-1980s, soybeans had become Louisiana's chief agricultural product.

Cattle ranchers still graze their herds in many areas of the state. About 10 percent of the state's cash farm income comes from the sale of beef cattle and calves. Louisiana also produces dairy products, eggs, chickens, and hogs.

NATURAL RESOURCES

Even in the late 1980s, thousands of men and women were still making their living from the bounty of Louisiana's forests, marshes, and coastal waters. Careful reforestation has replenished the forests of the north. About 15 million acres (6 million hectares) of pine forest in the north belong to timber companies, which cut the trees for sawmills and paper manufacturers. Each year, Bayou trappers sell the pelts of half a million muskrats and a million nutria. Fishermen along the Gulf coast haul in 2 billion pounds (.9 billion kilograms) of shrimp, menhaden, and redfish annually.

Louisiana is the nation's leading producer of salt, and is second only to Texas in sulfur mining. Natural gas, found in conjunction with petroleum, is a vital part of the state's economy. Yet more than any other mineral resource, it was oil that transformed the image of Louisiana in the twentieth century.

Since the first gusher came in at Jennings in 1901, it is estimated that Louisiana has produced 14 billion barrels of oil—enough to cover the entire land surface of the earth with an oil slick nine inches (twenty-three centimeters) thick. By the late 1970s, when

Some Louisiana drilling-crew workers are stationed in the Gulf on offshore rigs such as this one just south of the mouth of the Mississippi River.

oil sold on the world market for thirty-six dollars a barrel, more than a thousand wells operated throughout the state. Morgan City functioned as the land base for hundreds of offshore oil rigs stationed in the Gulf.

Louisiana's economy depended on oil and the related petrochemical industry. When the price of oil tumbled below twenty dollars per barrel in the mid-1980s, the results were devastating. Hundreds of oil wells stopped pumping, factories closed their doors, and unemployment soared. To make matters worse, geologists reported that Louisiana's remaining oil reserves might be exhausted by the first decade of the twenty-first century. Louisianians today face the sobering fact that their state can no longer rely on oil as the mainstay of its economy.

Louisiana factories produce fertilizers, medicines, soap, and paper. They manufacture aluminum and transportation equipment, and process sugar, rice, fruits, vegetables, and seafood. But all of these industries are still overshadowed by oil and its countless byproducts: gasoline, paints, plastics, chemicals, and even cosmetics. To create jobs and revenue in the future, Louisiana must diversify and find innovative ways to tap its natural and human resources.

Chapter 9

CULTURE AND RECREATION

CULTURE AND RECREATION

Laissez les bons temps rouller! goes an old Louisiana saying. "Let the good times roll!" Louisianians celebrate life with literature, art, music, sports, and fine food. Above all, they have a talent for partying. Any occasion, from a saint's day to a funeral, is reason enough to let the good times roll.

LITERATURE AND ART

Because most of Louisiana's earliest settlers came from France, most of the state's early literature was written in French. In 1777, a wealthy merchant and plantation owner named Julien Poydras Lallande published a long poem extolling the virtues of the Spanish governor, Bernardo de Gálvez. In 1845, a group of free persons of color in New Orleans published *Les Cenelles*, an anthology of love poems that was the first black poetry ever published in the United States.

After the Civil War, French gradually yielded to English both in everyday life and in literature. In 1879, outspoken New Orleans writer George Washington Cable helped launch an era of local color in American fiction with his collection of short stories, *Old Creole Days*. He depicted the foibles as well as the charms of his characters, and many leading Creole families were outraged. Cable alienated himself even further through some of his later novels, which were deeply sympathetic to the struggles of Louisiana's newly freed blacks. A social outcast, he eventually fled to

Massachusetts, leaving behind his beloved home state forever.

The same blend of affection and censure runs through the work of many of Louisiana's twentieth-century writers. In her short stories and her novel *Keepers of the House*, Shirley Ann Grau revealed the destructive power of racism. New Orleans-born playwright Lillian Hellman wrote about decaying southern gentility in such dramas as *The Little Foxes* and *Another Part of the Forest*. Pulitzer Prizewinning novelist Walker Percy of Covington mingles mysticism with reality in *The Moviegoer* and *The Second Coming*.

Louisiana has also inspired writers outside the state. Robert Penn Warren's novel *All the King's Men* was modeled on the life of Huey Long. Tennessee Williams' Pulitzer Prizewinning play *A Streetcar Named Desire* is set in New Orleans and focuses on Blanche DuBois, a southern woman tarnished by hard times.

Probably the best-known artist to work in Louisiana was French-born naturalist and painter John James Audubon. In the 1820s, Audubon tramped the woods of the Felicianas country north of Lake Pontchartrain, observing wild birds and bringing them to life on canvas. His paintings give modern viewers a glimpse into Louisiana's forests as they were before the coming of roads and sawmills.

Today some Louisiana painters turn to the riches of their cultural heritage for inspiration. Clementine Hunter of Melrose Plantation near Natchitoches has received international acclaim for her watercolors, which have a distinctive African flavor.

MUSIC

Because they lived in constant fear of slave uprisings, the French of early New Orleans forbade blacks to assemble in public places. Slaves could gather only on Sunday evenings between six and nine o'clock in a city park called Congo Square. There someone would play a homemade bass fiddle, while another musician would beat passionate rhythms on the bamboula, a drum made from a hollow log. The musicians would improvise, creating new tunes and rhythms as they played. The crowd would clap, stamp, and sing, flinging itself into the spirit of the music. The music played on those Sunday evenings in Congo Square planted the seeds for that uniquely American brand of music known as jazz.

Jazz fuses the rhythms of traditional African music with the haunting cadences of spirituals, the fierce strength of work songs, and the exuberance of brass-band marches. This new form of music emerged in Storeyville, a district of saloons and gambling-houses that operated legally in New Orleans from 1897 until 1917. In taverns and dance halls, jazz musicians improvised on trombone, bass, and cornet or trumpet, experimenting with startling new harmonies and a syncopated beat.

In 1917, a group of white musicians called the Original Dixieland Jazz Band cut the first jazz record. It became an overnight hit. In 1923, the Creole Jazz Band, a black group led by cornetist Joe "King" Oliver, made the first of a series of classic recordings. King Oliver's second trumpeter was destined to become one of the most influential jazz musicians in the world. His name was Louis Armstrong.

Daniel Louis Armstrong grew up in a tough, all-black section of New Orleans. When he was thirteen, he was sent to a detention home for firing a gun in the street. While he was serving his sentence, he learned to play the cornet. When he was released, he put his talent to work and began to play with jazz bands in and around Storeyville. He was in his early twenties when he left New

New Orleans-born Louis Armstrong (kneeling), who was to become one of the world's most famous jazz musicians, played in King Oliver's Creole Jazz Band in the early 1920s.

Orleans for Chicago with King Oliver's band. Soon he was leading his own band and making famous such numbers as "Cornet Chop Suey" and "West End Blues."

Louis Armstrong's riveting trumpet solos helped win jazz worldwide recognition as an art form. In his honor, and to commemorate the long-forgotten musicians who played there centuries before, Congo Square was renamed Louis Armstrong Plaza.

A very different form of music unique to Louisiana is the accordion music of the Cajuns. Groups of musicians travel from town to town performing at all-night dances called *fais-dodos* (literally, "go to sleep"). A Cajun band usually consists of a fiddle, guitar, accordion, and set of steel triangles. Many of the rollicking tunes came to the New World from France in the early 1700s. But the songs, though usually sung in French, are often distinctly American in theme. Even the vicious bayou mosquitoes are a worthy subject: "The mosquitoes have eaten up my sweetheart! They have left only two big toes!"

A number of musical traditions thrive in Louisiana, as is illustrated by (clockwise from top left) a fiddler at the Zydeco Festival in Plaisance, a folksinger at the Folklife Festival near Shreveport, a Cajun band at the Festival Acadiens in Lafayette, a classical concert in Baton Rouge, and jazz musicians at Preservation Hall in New Orleans.

While jazz and Cajun music enjoy widespread popularity, Louisianians appreciate classical music as well. The New Orleans Symphony is recognized throughout the nation. Other fine orchestras play at Shreveport, Baton Rouge, and Lake Charles. New Orleans is noted for its excellent opera productions and for a number of outstanding theaters.

SPORTS

Louisiana is a hunter's and fisherman's paradise. The bayous teem with bass and giant catfish. Vast flocks of ducks and geese winter along the Gulf coast, and its waters are filled with giant rays, tarpon, and pompano. Shrimp and oysters are also plentiful. Quail, doves, and deer are found in the fields and forests.

In competitive sports, too, Louisiana has earned high honors. The Fighting Tigers of Louisiana State University have been a formidable football team for more than half a century. Grambling State University, which has long been known as a producer of outstanding professional athletes, also has a leading football team. Grambling rose to fame in the 1960s through the unwavering determination of the team's remarkable coach, Eddie Robinson.

When Louisiana's vast indoor sports arena, the Superdome, opened in New Orleans in 1975, it was promoted as "a triumph of man's imagination." Critics grumble that the immense, twenty-seven-story bubble looks more like a UFO. It is so large that Houston's Astrodome could fit neatly inside. In addition to serving as home field for the NFL's New Orleans Saints, the Superdome hosts rock concerts and a variety of other sports events. By far the most popular is the annual Sugar Bowl, when a hopeful challenger confronts the leading college football team in the Southeastern Conference.

LOUISIANA CUISINE

A Louisianian died and went to heaven. As soon as he arrived, he asked Saint Peter if they served gumbo. When Saint Peter said no, he turned around and came straight back to Louisiana.

This old story reflects the importance of food in Louisiana life. Few other states have contributed such exotic recipes to American cuisine.

A visitor to Louisiana can sample the state's finest culinary delights on an eating tour of New Orleans. The city's French Quarter is world famous for such elegant restaurants as Antoine's, Arnaud's, and Commander's Palace. Food at more modest establishments can be just as memorable. As one traveler exclaimed, "You can't get served a bad hot dog in this town!"

The staple of southern Louisiana cookery is seafood—shrimp, oysters, redfish, catfish, and perhaps most renowned of all, the humble bayou crawfish. Generally under six inches in length, the crawfish is a relative of the lobster—but Louisianians claim it is far more delicious. It is served in such dishes as crawfish bisque (a light soup), and crawfish etouffé (crawfish smothered in onions and tomatoes and served over rice).

The Cajun specialty gumbo is a delectable stew that may contain shrimp, oysters, crabmeat, sausage, or any other meat the cook has handy. All are simmered to perfection with peppers, tomatoes, onions, and okra in a big cast-iron pot, seasoned with a zesty dash of hot tabasco sauce, and served over rice. Another Cajun treat is the rich chowder of rice and seafood called jambalaya.

Creole cooking harks back to the opulent days of the French and Spanish elite. Unlike the hardier Cajun fare, it relies on such ingredients as wine, orange peel, and saffron, and is served with a

The world-famous cuisine of southern Louisiana includes such dishes as grilled redfish (above), boiled crawfish (above right), and gumbo (right).

continental finesse. Typical Creole dishes are oysters Rockefeller (oysters with finely chopped spinach) and bouillabaisse (a fish soup with a tomato base).

The influence of neighboring Texas is evident in the food one encounters in the western uplands, where red beans and rice, Mexican hot tamales, and chili are specialties.

Perhaps the best way to sample Louisiana food is to attend one of the state's countless festivals, where food of every variety is served in abundance.

Among the many events unique to Louisiana are (clockwise from top left) Mardi Gras, shown here in New Orleans but celebrated throughout French Louisiana; Baton Rouge's Fest For All; the Pecan Festival in Colfax; and a New Orleans jazz funeral.

A PARTY FOR EVERY OCCASION

In Crowley, the rice capital of America, hundreds turn out every year for the town's famous rice festival. Plaquemines Parish holds an orange festival, while the people of St. Landry Parish honor the sweet potato at the "Yambilee" each October. New Orleans hosts a yearly Jazz and Heritage Festival, and the Christmas Festival in Natchitoches draws thousands of visitors.

The people of Louisiana have a talent for partying. Every harvest, holiday, or saint's day is cause for celebration. Even funerals sometimes turn into a time of revelry. At a traditional "jazz funeral," musicians play mournful dirges on the way to the cemetery, but break into rollicking marching tunes on the journey home. Louis Armstrong once remarked that he had played at so many funerals, he no longer feared death.

Shrove Tuesday, or Mardi Gras, is a colorful annual event celebrated throughout much of French Louisiana. But nowhere is the festival more spectacular than in New Orleans. Mardi Gras, the Tuesday before Ash Wednesday and the start of Lent, was first celebrated in Louisiana by French colonists in the early 1700s. Today, the Mardi Gras season begins with a series of parties and balls on Twelfth Night, January 6. For nearly two months, the city rocks with music and dancing. Colorful street parades begin the week before Mardi Gras Day, culminating in a wild carnival extravaganza on the night of Mardi Gras itself.

Mardi Gras has sometimes been described as "the greatest free show on earth." Every year, more than a million revelers from all over the world pour through the streets of New Orleans, most of them disguised by plumed, sequined costumes and outlandish masks. A parade of floats adorned in the Mardi Gras colors— purple for royalty, gold for wealth, and green for faith—winds through the packed streets. The floats mark their progress with a series of "throws" and "catches." With every throw, the people on the floats toss brightly colored Mardi Gras beads and mock Spanish gold coins or doubloons to the eager bystanders. With every "catch," people scramble, shouting and laughing, to grab souvenirs of the Mardi Gras excitement. For the hundreds of thousands of people who flock to New Orleans in the weeks before Ash Wednesday, Mardi Gras is a chance to live the spirit of the old French saying, "*Laissez les bon temps rouller!*" "Let the good times roll!"

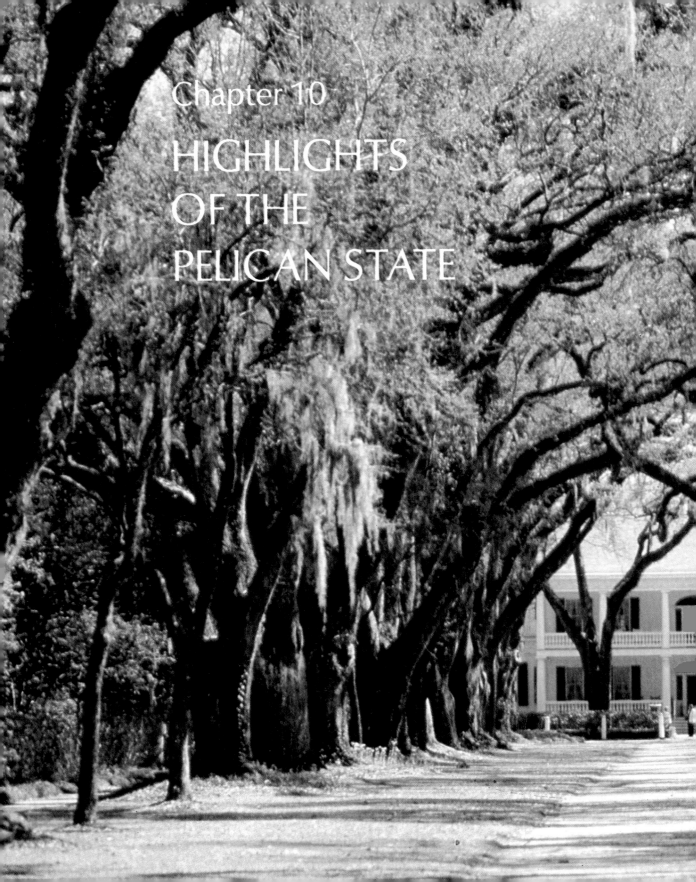

Chapter 10

HIGHLIGHTS OF THE PELICAN STATE

HIGHLIGHTS OF THE PELICAN STATE

Sometimes a baker in French Louisiana will toss in an extra croissant when a customer asks for a dozen. When you pay for a pound of pralines, the owner of the candy store may add a few more as a surprise. This custom is called giving *lagniappe*, "a little something extra."

Louisiana has a delightful way of giving something extra to the visitor. On a tour of the state that goes from the wetlands to the rolling pine hills and then back down the Mississippi River to New Orleans, the charm of the scenery is enhanced by intriguing bits of history. Everywhere there is music to hear, exotic new dishes to sample, festivals to enjoy. At each turn in the road, Louisiana offers a gift of *lagniappe*.

SOUTHERN LOUISIANA

"This place [the Atchafalaya Swamp] is like no other," a sports fisherman from Baton Rouge told a *National Geographic* reporter. "I come out here to get away from the city, to revive my mind. Everywhere else you go it's crowded, but it's not crowded here."

In the vast swamp that stretches along the Atchafalaya River from the Red River to the Gulf, the stillness is broken only by the cries of birds, and now and then the rumbling call of a giant bullfrog. Tangled beards of Spanish moss stream from live oaks and twisted cypresses. The brackish waters of ponds and wandering bayous abound with bass, catfish, shad, and crawfish.

**The slow-moving
waters of a bayou in
southern Louisiana**

The swamp is home to the muskrat, heron, and alligator, and man
seems out of place.

Yet, even in this wilderness, civilization has brought shattering
changes. To prevent disastrous floods along the Mississippi, a
sprawling system of gates and spillways channels floodwater
through the swamp into the Atchafalaya River. Dozens of gas and
oil pipelines crisscross the swamp, and canals and service roads
cut it into ever smaller pieces. Some environmentalists fear that
the delicate ecology of the Atchafalaya Swamp, and of all the
wetlands in south Louisiana, have suffered irreparable damage.

Southern Louisiana is sometimes referred to as "Cajun country"
because of the strong Acadian influence there. The Acadians are
mainly a rural people. But they tend to subdivide their land so
that every child can inherit a portion, and with each generation

95

The Evangeline Oak (left) and statue (right) in St. Martinville commemorate Longfellow's famous poem *Evangeline.*

their houses become more and more crowded together. It is said that one could throw a baseball from house to house for 100 miles (161 kilometers) along Bayou Lafourche from Donaldsonville to the Gulf of Mexico.

One of the surprises Louisiana holds for visitors is a French cowboy tradition. Louisiana ranches are known as *vacheries.* The cowhands herding the cattle that graze on the Attakapas prairies are more likely to be named Pierre or Jacques than Tex or Slim. From 1739 until 1954, all of the cattle brands in the state were registered in the French Brand Book, kept in the St. Martinville courthouse.

Near Bayou Teche in St. Martinville towers the ancient, massive tree known as the Evangeline Oak. Outside nearby St. Martin de Tours Church stands a statue of the young Acadian woman who,

Authentic nineteenth-century Acadian architecture can be seen at Acadian Village in Lafayette.

in Longfellow's poem, waited in vain for her lost lover. The story of Evangeline has come to symbolize the patience and unflagging loyalty of the Acadian spirit.

Between Bayou Teche and the Calcasieu River, thousands of acres of Louisiana prairie are flooded for rice cultivation. As a secondary industry, some enterprising farmers raise crawfish in the ponds that cover the rice fields. True to Louisiana tradition, an annual rice festival is celebrated in Crowley, the "rice capital of America." To rollicking accordion music, the Rice Queen flings bags of rice from her float to the cheering crowds below.

The older section of Lafayette, with its churches, gardens, and narrow, winding streets, has all the charm of a French cathedral

Left: St. John the Evangelist Church in Lafayette
Above: Oil-drilling equipment being transported on
the Intracoastal Waterway near Morgan City

town. But another Lafayette has sprung up beyond downtown—a
dizzying complex of hotels and high-rise office buildings. Some
eight hundred oil-related companies had their Louisiana
headquarters in Lafayette in the late 1970s. Ten years later, with
the slump in oil prices, many of these buildings stood empty.

Since the late nineteenth century, Morgan City had been the
hub of Louisiana's shrimp-fishing industry. But in 1947, when
underwater drilling struck oil beneath the Gulf, Morgan City
became the capital of the state's offshore oil industry as well. The
constant activity disrupted the shrimp beds, while pollution from
oil spills caused untold destruction. The shrimp catch declined
year by year, and many lifelong shrimpers were driven out of
business. This situation began to change, however, when the oil
industry lost momentum. Ironically, as the shrimp returned, they
gathered in great numbers around the abandoned oil rigs.

The influence of early French and Spanish settlers is still charmingly apparent in Natchitoches.

THE UPLANDS

North of the prairie, the land rises gradually to form low, rolling, pine-covered hills. In the central part of the state, a visitor can find evidence of three of the cultures that have contributed to Louisiana's ethnic heritage. Outside Marksville, a cluster of earthen burial mounds stand as silent reminders of some of Louisiana's earliest inhabitants. Along the Cane River is the Isle Brevelle country, where free people of color became wealthy cotton planters years before the Civil War. To the west of this region, the town of Zwolle holds an annual tamale festival that recalls the days when Mexico claimed the land along the Sabine River.

On the Red River stands the city of Natchitoches. Founded in 1714, Natchitoches is the oldest continuously occupied settlement in Louisiana. It is also one of the few places in the northern part of the state where the influence of the early French and Spanish is still charmingly apparent. In the national historic district at the

Shreveport, Louisiana's third-largest city, lies on the Red River in the northwestern corner of the state.

heart of the town, balconies with wrought-iron railings overlook narrow brick streets, and wooden doors are carved with intricate floral designs. Many painters have been drawn to Natchitoches and the surrounding countryside, where roads wander through stately groves of pecan trees and magnolia blossoms perfume the air.

Until 1837, the Red River beyond Natchitoches was completely blocked by the Red River Raft, an enormous tangle of sunken logs and branches that stretched for hundreds of miles into Arkansas and Oklahoma. In 1833, the government commissioned Captain Henry Miller Shreve, an engineer, to clear the river for navigation, a remarkable project that took nearly seven years to complete. Shreve opened northwestern Louisiana to settlement and trade, and in 1837 founded the city that still bears his name — Shreveport. By the mid-1800s, Shreveport was the hub of the cotton industry in northwestern Louisiana. According to one account, "the very streets and sidewalks were piled and cluttered with bales." Shreveport is proud of its fine symphony orchestra, its art galleries, and its theaters. Of special interest is the R.W. Norton Art Gallery, which boasts the Southeast's largest collection of paintings from the American West.

Monroe's attractions include the Masur Museum of Art (left); and Elsong Gardens, which features a collection of Coca-Cola memorabilia (above).

The largest city in northeastern Louisiana is Monroe, located on the Ouachita River near the Arkansas border. Visitors to Monroe are impressed by the city's gleaming downtown civic center—a complex that includes a theater, a convention hall, and the nationally acclaimed Masur Museum of Art. The people of Monroe are especially proud of the Elsong Gardens, where visitors can wander for hours, bathed in the fragrance and dazzling colors of hundreds of exotic flowering plants. The gardens were the creation of operatic singer Emmie Lou Biedenharn, whose father, Joseph Biedenharn, was the first bottler of Coca-Cola. On the grounds is a small museum of antique bottles and other Coca-Cola memorabilia.

DOWN THE MISSISSIPPI

Rolling toward the Gulf with a slow, irresistible power, the dark-brown waters of the Mississippi River shaped much of Louisiana's human history, and molded the very land itself. A journey down the river to the delta is an expedition into the past, and an excursion into the hive of industry and culture that is Louisiana today.

In the north, the river serves as the boundary between Louisiana and its eastern neighbor, Mississippi. Where the upper part of the toe of the Louisiana boot juts to the east, the Mississippi flows entirely within the state. To the east lie the lovely wooded hills of West and East Feliciana parishes, where John James Audubon painted wild birds in the 1820s. Pointe Coupee Parish, site of some of the oldest of Louisiana's great plantation houses, lies to the west.

Farther to the south, the river glides past Louisiana's bustling capital, Baton Rouge. In English, the French phrase *baton rouge* means "red stick." The city takes its name from the tall red pole that once stood at the river's edge to mark the boundary of the Houma Indians' hunting grounds. Seven flags have flown over Baton Rouge since its founding in the eighteenth century: the flags of France, Great Britain, Spain, the short-lived Republic of West Florida, the United States, the Confederacy, and finally, the United States again.

Though it is about 235 miles (378 kilometers) from the Gulf, Baton Rouge is the fourth-busiest port in the nation, and one of the busiest inland ports in the world. The nation's tallest state capitol building, commissioned by Governor Huey P. Long, towers thirty-four stories above the downtown streets.

Since the state's first oil refinery opened there in 1909, Baton Rouge has stood at the heart of Louisiana's petroleum industry. Below the city, the river surges through a landscape of oil tanks and smokestacks that stretches for 80 miles (129 kilometers) to New Orleans. Yet here and there around the river's unexpected twists and turns, elegant plantation houses stand as living relics of the splendid, tragic days that led to the Civil War. Many, such as

West Feliciana Parish
Pointe Coupee Parish
East Feliciana Parish
★ Baton Rouge
New Orleans

Left: the Old State Capitol in Baton Rouge
Above: Nottoway Plantation, the largest antebellum plantation home in the South

San Francisco House, Nottoway House, and Houmas House, have been fully restored and are open to the public.

The brackish waters of Lake Pontchartrain come within a few scant miles of the Mississippi. Teeming with shrimp, oysters and fish, the lake furnishes much of the seafood that graces the tables of New Orleans. Thousands of acres along the lakeshore have been designated as recreation areas or wildlife preserves. In the lovely Fountainebleau State Park near Mandeville, visitors can explore the ruins of an 1829 sugar mill and hike for miles through a stately forest of oak, sweet gum, and magnolia.

On flows the river, straining against its levees, to the pride of Louisiana—the dazzling city of New Orleans.

THE CRESCENT CITY

"It was one of the most unlikely spots on earth to build a city," wrote the late Louisiana congressman Hale Boggs. "It was literally on a swamp, mostly below sea level, with floods and hurricanes and every pestilence known to man." Despite all these drawbacks, Governor Bienville chose the site for its strategic military position. In 1718, he authorized construction of the new city on a crescent-shaped spit of land nestled between Lake Pontchartrain and a curve in the Mississippi. Although the city soon swelled beyond the original section, New Orleans is still often referred to as the Crescent City.

A walk through the narrow streets of the original section, known as the French Quarter, is a delight to the senses. Wrought-iron balconies lean above the narrow streets, and many windows are adorned with pots of flowers. Mingled aromas float from open doorways—limes and oranges, frying shrimp, jasmine blossoms from some inner courtyard. Street musicians fill the air with the competing strains of jazz, Cajun music, country, and rock. In the evenings, jazz connoisseurs pack the restaurants and clubs along Bourbon Street that feature live entertainment. No food or beverages are served at world-famous Preservation Hall, yet crowds gather for an hour before the doors open, eager to hear the finest jazz performers New Orleans can offer. The perfect ending to a true New Orleans-style evening is a visit to one of the coffee houses in the Old French Market. There one can sit and relax, sipping coffee flavored with chicory and munching on *beignets* (puffy, square doughnuts covered with powdered sugar), while watching the people go by.

Clustered around Jackson Square are several state museums that commemorate the history of New Orleans and the contributions it

A visitor's day
in New Orleans
(above left)
might include
(clockwise from
above right) a
river cruise on
the steamboat
Natchez, a tour
of the Garden
District via the
St. Charles Ave.
streetcar, a
visit to a flea
market, a walk
through the
historic French
Quarter, and a
stop for coffee
and beignets at
the French Market.

New Orleans' early cemeteries (above) had to be built aboveground because the city's location made it vulnerable to flooding. The Cabildo in Jackson Square (right), now a museum, was the seat of government when the Louisiana colony was under Spanish rule.

has made to American culture. The Cabildo, once the center of government under Spanish rule, houses a treasure trove of historical documents and exhibits, including Indian artifacts. Displays in the old United States Mint Building trace jazz from its origins to the present. In the middle of Jackson Square, the great bronze statue of Andrew Jackson sits astride his rearing horse.

Beyond the French Quarter, New Orleans has all the bustle and noise of any other modern city. The business district bristles with high-rise office buildings, and traffic clogs the streets. New Orleans has its share of poverty, too. Desire, the section of town made famous by Tennessee Williams' play, is a sprawling slum along the river, cut off from the city's mainstream by railroad tracks and canals. Today the site of a housing project, Desire is impoverished and crime-ridden, a study in the bleakest aspects of urban life.

"This is a fantastically strange town," commented Helen Mervis, a prominent New Orleans civic leader. " . . . There's a kind of ambivalence one has to have to live [here]. We have great tolerance for many things, good and bad. . . . And never forget that New Orleans is a carnival city."

In keeping with an old French and Spanish tradition, families meet and socialize among the tombs of their departed in New Orleans' cemeteries on November 1, All Saints Day. On St. Patrick's Day, thousands of green-clad revelers turn out for an exuberant parade in tribute to the city's large Irish population. Two days later, on March 19, the city's Italian community celebrates St. Joseph's Day by erecting altars laden with fresh fruits, vegetables, and pastries. These festivals and traditions are deeply rooted in the cultural and ethnic heritages of the respective groups. The grandest extravaganza of all is Mardi Gras, when the entire populace takes to the streets, throwing their inhibitions to the winds. At any time of year, New Orleans is sure to give the visitor a bit of *lagniappe*, "a little something extra."

Year by year, the face of Louisiana is changing. Rural roads are being paved, and paved roads are being widened into highways. As people from all over the country flock to Louisiana to visit or stay and work, Louisianians stream out to explore the rest of the nation. With this interchange of people and ideas, regional distinctions begin to blur. Yet as Louisiana strides toward the next century, its blend of cultures remains unique, and the spirit of its people is still irrepressible.

FACTS AT A GLANCE

GENERAL INFORMATION

Statehood: April 30, 1812, eighteenth state

Origin of Name: Named in honor of King Louis XIV by French explorer Sieur de La Salle, who claimed the Mississippi Valley region for France in 1682

State Capital: Baton Rouge, founded 1719

State Nickname: The "Pelican State"

State Flag: The state flag was adopted in 1912. It shows a white pelican nurturing three of its young in the center of a blue field. The state motto, "Union, Justice, and Confidence," is proclaimed on a white banner below the grouping.

State Motto: "Union, Justice, and Confidence"

State Bird: Eastern brown pelican

State Flower: Magnolia

State Tree: Bald cypress

State Insect: Honeybee

State Gem: Agate

State Song: Louisiana has two official state songs: "Give Me Louisiana," by Doralice Fontane, adopted in 1970; and the popular song "You Are My Sunshine," by Jimmie Davis (a governor of Louisiana) and Charles Mitchell, adopted in 1977:

GIVE ME LOUISIANA

Give me Louisiana, the State where I was born,
The State of snowy cotton, the best I've ever known,
A State of sweet magnolias and Creole melodies,
Oh give me Louisiana, the State where I was born.
Oh what sweet old mem'ries the mossy old oaks bring,
It brings us the story of our Evangeline.
A State of old tradition, of old plantation days,
Makes good old Louisiana the sweetest of all States.

Give me Louisiana, the State prepared to share,
That good old Southern custom, hospitality so rare,
A State of fruit and flowers, of sunshine and spring showers,
Oh give me Louisiana, the State where I was born.
Its woodlands, its marshes, where humble trappers live,
Its rivers, its valleys, a place to always give.
A State where work is pleasure, with blessings in full measure,
Makes good old Louisiana the dearest of all States.

Give me Louisiana, where love birds always sing,
In shady lanes or pastures, the cowbells softly ring,
The softness of the sunset brings peace and blissful rest,
Oh give me Louisiana, the State where I was born.
The smell of sweet clover, which blossoms ev'rywhere,
The fresh new mown hay, where children romp and play.
A State of love and laughter, a State for all here after,
Makes good old Louisiana the grandest of all States.

YOU ARE MY SUNSHINE

The other night dear, as I lay sleeping,
I dreamed I held you in my arms,
When I awoke dear, I was mistaken,
and I hung my head and cried:

Chorus:
You are my sunshine, my only sunshine,
you make me happy when skies are gray.
You'll never know dear, how much I love you,
Please don't take my sunshine away.

I'll always love you, and make you happy,
if you will only say the same,
But if you leave me to love another,
you'll regret it all some day:

(Chorus)

You told me once dear, you really loved me,
And no one else could come between,
but now you've left me and love another,
you have shattered all my dreams:

(Chorus)

POPULATION

Population: 4,206,312, nineteenth among the states (1980 census)

Population Density: 94.5 people per sq. mi. (36.5 people per km^2)

Population Distribution: 68.6 percent urban, 31.4 percent rural

New Orleans	557,927
Baton Rouge	219,486
Shreveport	205,820
Lafayette	81,961
Lake Charles	75,226
Kenner	66,382
Monroe	57,597
Alexandria	51,564
Bossier City	50,817

(Population figures according to 1980 census)

Population Growth: Louisiana's population increased greatly in the early 1900s with the development of the state's vast resources of oil, natural gas, and timber. In the mid-1900s, jobs created by new technology in the petrochemical and timber industries brought about another significant population increase. From 1970 to 1980, the state's population grew by a healthy 15.5 percent, compared to the national population-growth rate of 11.45 percent. However, that growth slowed in the mid-1980s because of the decline in the oil and gas industry.

Year	Population
1820	153,407
1840	352,411
1860	708,002
1880	939,946
1900	1,381,625
1920	1,798,509
1940	2,363,880
1950	2,683,516
1960	3,257,022
1970	3,644,637
1980	4,206,312

GEOGRAPHY

Borders: States that border Louisiana are Arkansas on the north, Mississippi on the east, and Texas on the west. The Gulf of Mexico determines Louisiana's southern boundary.

Highest Point: Driskill Mountain in Bienville Parish, 535 ft. (163 m)

Lowest Point: New Orleans, 5 ft. (1.5 m) below sea level

Greatest Distances: North to south—237 mi. (381.3 km)
East to west—236.5 mi. (380.5 km)

Area: 47,752 sq. mi. (123,682 km²), including 3,400 sq. mi. (8,806 km²) of inland water. Louisiana's actual area changes from week to week as river and tidal waters overflow and recede, covering or exposing land area.

Rank in Area Among the States: Thirty-first

Rivers: The Mississippi River dominates the state. From its headwaters in the northern United States to its mouth at the Gulf of Mexico, the river is 2,348 mi. (3,778 km) long; nearly 600 mi. (965.4 km) of the lower Mississippi are in Louisiana. As it flows through the land, the Mississippi accumulates a great amount of silt (fine soil particles), much of which it has deposited near the river's mouth to form the great Mississippi Delta. The delta covers about 13,000 sq. mi. (33,670 km²), almost one-fourth of Louisiana's area.

The river also deposits silt throughout its course to the Gulf. Consequently, away from the river, the land slopes down to form low-lying backlands. Flooding is a serious concern. Levees (man-made walls) built along the rivers help control flooding. There are some 1,650 mi. (2,655 km) of levees in Louisiana. Other man-made flood controls include the Bonnet Carré and Morganza spillways on the Mississippi River; and the Atchafalaya Floodway on the Atchafalaya River, which can be opened to carry off high waters. Other important rivers in the state are the Red, Ouachita, Sabine, Pearl, Calcasieu, and Black. Louisiana is famous for its bayous. A bayou is generally a small river, but it can be any small, slow-moving inlet or outlet of a lake or of the sea itself. Most bayous are former mouths of the Mississippi River. Among Louisiana's chief bayous are the Teche, Lafourche, Macon, Boeuf, Dorcheat, and D'Arbonne.

Lakes: Lake Pontchartrain, the state's largest lake with an area of 625 sq. mi. (1,619 km²), is a brackish (part saltwater) lake. Coastal lagoons of note include Calcasieu Lake, White Lake, and Lake Borgne. Many small oxbow (crescent-shaped) freshwater lakes have been formed from meanderings of the Mississippi. Other freshwater lakes, including Caddo, Bistineau, and Black, were formed in the Red River Valley when the Red River was dammed off. Toledo Bend Reservoir, a man-made lake along the Louisiana-Texas border, has an area of 284 sq. mi. (736 km²). Coastal marshlands cover about 3,250 sq. mi. (8,418 km²) of Louisiana, but the actual amount of land under water changes constantly.

Topography: Louisiana lies wholly within the three main regions of the Gulf Coastal Plain, a fertile lowland that runs along the Gulf of Mexico from Florida to southern Texas. The area of the state east of the Mississippi River and north of Lake Pontchartrain is part of the East Gulf Coastal Plain. The floodplain and great delta of the lower Mississippi River are part of the Mississippi Alluvial Plain. The West Gulf Coastal Plain includes all of Louisiana west of the Mississippi.

From a height of only some 500 ft. (152.4 m) in the hills of the north-central area, the state slopes down, following the Mississippi River, to sea level at the coastal marshlands in the south. The floodplains along the courses of the Mississippi, Red, and Ouachita rivers occupy about a third of the state. Rolling bluffs called

Cypress trees along Caddo Lake in northeastern Louisiana

frontlands follow the rivers and slope down away from them, forming silt-rich backlands. Farmland here is rich and productive. Just below an imaginary line connecting Franklin and Donaldsonville, the floodplain begins to widen to form the great Mississippi Delta.

Beyond the alluvial floodplains, in the area west and north of the Mississippi, and in the area east of the Mississippi and north of Lake Pontchartrain, are the hilly uplands. South of the northwestern uplands, a 60-mi.- (96.6-km-) wide belt of low-lying prairies stretches west from the Alluvial Plain to the state border. The prairies are noted for farm crops, especially rice, as well as ranching.

The coastal wetlands follow the Louisiana coastline, extending 20-30 mi. (32-48 km) inland. Including bays, river mouths, and some 2,500 coastal islands, the coastline measures 7,721 mi. (12,423 km). Alaska and Florida are the only states that have longer coastlines.

Climate: Louisiana's climate is hot, humid, and subtropical. It is one of the nation's wettest states, with an average annual precipitation of 56 in. (142 cm). Most of the precipitation is rainfall. In the southern part of the state, snow is rare; in the northern part, a few inches is considered a heavy snowfall. In January, temperatures range from an average of 55°F. (13°C) in the south, to an average of 49°F. (9°C) in the north. July temperatures average about 82°F. (28°C) in both the north and the south. The lowest temperature recorded in the state was -16°F. (-27°C) at Minden on February 13, 1899. The highest recorded temperature in the state was 114°F. (46°C) at Plain Dealing on August 10, 1936.

NATURE

Trees: Magnolia, oak, cypress, sweet gum, hickory, loblolly pine, longleaf pine, shortleaf pine, slash pine, eastern red cedar, beech, black walnut

Wild Plants: Iris, honeysuckle, jasmine, violet, Spanish dagger, lily, hibiscus and other mallows, passionflower, Spanish moss, azalea, camellia, many orchid species, pitcher plant (an insect-trapping plant), yellow lotus, water hemlock, water hyacinth

Animals: White-tailed deer, squirrels, eastern cottontail rabbits, swamp rabbits, gray foxes, weasels, raccoons, nutrias, Louisiana muskrats, mink, opossums, skunks, wild hogs, bobcats, otters, and beavers; coastal and marine animals include alligators, sea turtles, and, seen offshore, dolphins

Birds: Half the ducks and geese in North America winter along the Louisiana coast. Other birds that can be found in the state include quail, wild turkey, woodcocks, doves, brown thrashers, chickadees, crows, hawks, owls, herons, swifts, warblers, purple martins, hummingbirds, egrets, storks, cranes, swans, brown pelicans, bald eagles, and red-cockaded woodpeckers.

Fish: Freshwater fish include bass, bream, catfish, crappie, drumfish, and sunfish; coastal and marine fish and shellfish include giant rays, menhaden, pompano, tarpon, bluefish, redfish, flounder, Spanish mackerel, speckled trout, shrimp, oysters, and crawfish.

GOVERNMENT

The government of Louisiana, like the federal government, is divided into three branches—legislative, executive, and judicial. The state's legislature is made up of a senate with 39 members and a house of representatives with 105 members. The legislature creates new laws, rescinds or revises old ones, and works with the governor to prepare the state budget. It also has the power to impeach and remove judicial and executive officials. The state senate can refuse to confirm certain appointments made by the governor. Voters elect both state senators and state representatives to terms of four years.

The executive branch, headed by the governor, administers the law. The governor may serve an unlimited number of terms, but no more than two terms in a row. The state constitution gives the governor the authority to veto or approve laws passed by the legislature, to grant pardons, to serve as commander-in-chief of the state militia, and to call emergency sessions of the legislature. The governor also has the power to appoint the heads of many state departments, subject to approval by the state senate.

The judicial branch interprets laws and tries cases. The state has four kinds of courts—supreme, appellate, district, and a number of lesser courts. The highest court, the supreme court, hears both civil and criminal cases. It has a chief justice and six associate justices. All are elected to ten-year terms. The associate justice with the longest service becomes the chief justice. There are four courts of appeal and thirty-three district courts. Louisiana is the only state that does not follow the English common-law system whereby judges base their rulings on previous court decisions. Instead, in most civil cases, they rely largely on a body of written laws based on the Napoleonic Code of France. In criminal matters, a combination of code and common law is used.

Number of Counties: Louisiana is the only state that calls its counties parishes. There are sixty-four parishes.

U.S. Representatives: 8

Electoral Votes: 10

Voting Qualifications: Eighteen years of age, one year residency in state, and six months residency in parish.

EDUCATION

Louisiana ranks thirty-eighth among the states in annual expenditure on education per pupil. There are about 1,955 elementary and secondary schools in Louisiana; nearly one out of every three is private. The Roman Catholic church runs the largest number of private schools.

Louisiana has thirty-two institutions of higher learning; twelve of them are private. Louisiana State University (LSU) at Baton Rouge is the heart of the state's university system. It also has campuses at Alexandria, Eunice, and Shreveport. Other state-run universities are Louisiana Tech University in Ruston, Southern University in Baton Rouge (with branch campuses at New Orleans and Shreveport), the University of Southwestern Louisiana in Lafayette, Grambling State University in Grambling, Southeastern Louisiana University in Hammond, Northwestern State University in Natchitoches, Francis T. Nicholls State University in Thibodaux, McNeese State University in Lake Charles, Northeast Louisiana University in Monroe, and Delgado College in New Orleans. Louisiana's largest private institution of higher learning, Tulane University in New Orleans, is one of the most prestigious schools in the South. Other private institutions include Loyola University of New Orleans, Xavier University of Louisiana at New Orleans, Louisiana College in Pineville, and Centenary College of Louisiana in Shreveport.

ECONOMY AND INDUSTRY

Principal Products:
Agriculture: Soybeans, sweet potatoes, rice, sugarcane, pecans, cotton, corn, clover, white potatoes, hay, wheat, alfalfa, melons, strawberries, citrus fruits, beans, cabbage, peppers, tomatoes, beef cattle, poultry and eggs, dairy products, hogs, forest products
Manufacturing: Chemicals, petroleum products, processed food, lumber and wood products, paper, apparel, transportation equipment, fabricated metals

Sugarcane, one of Louisiana's most important crops, is grown mainly in the south-central part of the state.

Natural Resources: Natural gas, petroleum, salt, sulfur, fertile soil, sand, gravel, lime, shell, clay, stone, gypsum, forests, fish, shellfish, game birds and animals, muskrat and nutria fur

Business and Industry: The mining and processing of minerals is one of the most important aspects of Louisiana's economy. Among the states, Louisiana is second only to Texas in mineral production. The mining of the state's abundant deposits of petroleum, natural gas, salt, and sulfur accounts for almost 20 percent of Louisiana's gross state product (the total value of all goods and services produced in a year). Chemical manufacturing is Louisiana's most important industry, followed by the manufacturing of coal and petroleum products. Service industries play a major role in the state's economy, accounting for 60 percent of the gross state product. Service industries include wholesale and retail trade; community, social, and personal services; and the services associated with tourism, such as hotels, restaurants, and entertainment. Nearly three million tourists visit the state each year, spending a total of nearly $3.5 billion.

Communication: Louisiana has 25 daily newspapers and about 85 weeklies. The major daily newspaper in New Orleans is the *Times-Picayune/States-Item*, which has the largest circulation in the state. The *Louisiana Weekly*, also published in New Orleans, is one of the South's most important black-oriented newspapers. Other important dailies are Shreveport's *Times*, the *Baton Rouge Advocate*, the *Alexandria Town Talk*, Monroe's *Daily World* and *News-Star*, and the *Lake Charles American Press*. Louisiana has 170 radio stations and some 20 commercial television stations.

Transportation: The Mississippi River has always played a central role in the Louisiana transportation system. Today, oceangoing boats can sail upriver all the way to Baton Rouge—350 mi. (563 km) by water from the Gulf of Mexico. The Gulf Intracoastal Waterway, which stretches all the way across Louisiana along the coastal marshes, is the state's only east-west waterway. It provides sheltered passage for tugboats and barges. The port of New Orleans serves about five thousand ships each year, and handles more cargo than any other port in the United States. A direct route between New Orleans and the Gulf is provided by the 76-mi.- (122-km-) long Mississippi River/Gulf Outlet. Baton Rouge, the nation's fourth-busiest port, is important for the shipping of petroleum products.

The Lake Pontchartrain Causeway, opened in 1956, is the longest bridge in the world. The Huey P. Long Bridge, which crosses the Mississippi north of New Orleans, was opened in 1935. Other bridges cross the Mississippi at Baton Rouge, Donaldsonville, Vidalia, in Madison Parish, and in New Orleans. The state's newest major bridge is the Hale Boggs. It crosses the Mississippi River upriver from New Orleans between Luling and Destrehan.

There are 55,000 mi. (88,495 km) of roads and highways in Louisiana. The state has 290 airports, and is served by 15 airlines. New Orleans Moisant International Airport is the state's largest airport. There are 4,000 mi. (6,436 km) of railroad track in the state.

SOCIAL AND CULTURAL LIFE

Museums: The state's largest museum is the Louisiana State Museum, a complex of eight historic buildings in the French Quarter of New Orleans. Seven of the buildings are open to the public, including the Cabildo, the center of government under Spanish rule; the 1850 House, a beautifully restored example of a nineteenth-century home; Jackson House; Madame John's Legacy, a classic example of colonial Creole architecture; the Old U.S. Mint, which houses the New Orleans Jazz Museum and the Mardi Gras Museum; the Arsenal, which served as a prison during Spanish rule; and the Presbytère, which was built in 1793 as a residence for priests and now houses natural-history exhibits. Also of interest in New Orleans are the Confederate Museum, the Lamp Gallery, and the Louisiana Military History and State Weapons Museum. The New Orleans Museum of Art and the R.W. Norton Art Gallery in Shreveport house extensive collections. The Louisiana State Exhibit Museum in Shreveport presents the story of Louisiana's industries, wildlife, and natural resources. The Louisiana Arts and Science Center in Baton Rouge features a planetarium, as well as history and wildlife displays. The Museum of Natural Science at Louisiana State University is one of the outstanding museums of its kind in the United States. The Brimstone Museum in Sulphur offers films and exhibits about Louisiana's sulfur industry. Other interesting museums include the Oil and Gas Park in Jennings, the Rice Museum in Crowley, the Bayou Folk Museum in Cloutierville, the Rural Life Museum in Baton Rouge, and the Meadows Museum of Indochinese Art at Centenary College in Shreveport.

Libraries: The library at Louisiana State University, with over one million volumes, is the state's largest. The New Orleans Public Library has eleven branches and 802,934 volumes, and houses a special collection of jazz and folk music. The Louisiana State Museum and the Howard Library, both in New Orleans, have extensive collections on the history of Louisiana. Tulane University's library is strong in the subjects of jazz and Louisiana history. Grambling State University, Southern University at Baton Rouge, and Xavier University of Louisiana at New Orleans all have special collections in black studies. Northwestern State University at Natchitoches has special collections on Louisiana folklore, Indians, plants, and oral history.

Performing Arts: The New Orleans Philharmonic Symphony is the state's leading symphony orchestra. Baton Rouge, Alexandria, and Lake Charles also have

The Louisiana Superdome in New Orleans, home of the NFL New Orleans Saints, is the world's largest indoor stadium.

symphony orchestras. There are opera companies in New Orleans, Shreveport, and Baton Rouge. The New Orleans Ballet performs at the Theatre of the Performing Arts. Theatergoers in New Orleans can see plays at Le Petit Theatre du Vieux Carré, at Tulane University's Center Stage, at various dinner clubs, and at the Dashiki Project Theater. Outside of New Orleans, many cities and towns have their own amateur theater groups.

New Orleans, the "cradle" of jazz, is renowned for its many jazz clubs. Some of the most famous are Preservation Hall, Maison Bourbon, the Paddock Lounge, and the Famous Door. Cajun music, unique to Louisiana, has become increasingly popular in recent years. Musicians performing Cajun music commonly appear at folk festivals all over the nation. Black Cajun music, known as zydeco, has recently begun to receive national recognition.

Sports and Recreation: The New Orleans Saints of the National Football League play in the Superdome, a 74,726-seat indoor stadium that hosted the Superbowl in 1976 and 1985. The Sugar Bowl, held in the Superdome, is one of the nation's oldest and most prestigious college-bowl games. Thoroughbred and quarterhorse racing can be enjoyed at six major racetracks, including Louisiana Downs in Shreveport, the South's largest Thoroughbred racetrack.

Louisiana is a sportsman's paradise. The most popular fishing spots in the state are in the huge Toledo Bend Reservoir on the Louisiana-Texas border, the great Atchafalaya Swamp, Caddo Lake near Shreveport, and Catahoula Lake near Alexandria. Offshore fishing in the Gulf has actually improved since the establishment of Louisiana's offshore oil rigs, because the rigs act as artificial reefs and attract trophy-sized fish in large numbers. Grand Isle is the most popular spot for offshore and surf fishing. Louisiana's thirty-seven wildlife management areas provide excellent hunting. Canoeing is possible in Louisiana's beautiful man-made lagoons, as well as in the hundreds of rivers and streams throughout the state.

Louisiana maintains twelve state parks, seventeen state commemorative areas, and one state preservation area. Some of the more interesting state parks are Fountainebleau State Park near Mandeville, which features the ruins of a plantation brickyard and sugarmill; St. Bernard State Park; Lake Bruin State Park; and Grand Isle State Park, a 140-acre (56.7-hectare) site that offers marvelous swimming and fishing. Other popular state parks are Fairview-Riverside, Lake Bistineau, Sam Houston Jones, and Chicot state parks. Kisatchie National Forest is a

Hodges Gardens is a beautiful "garden in the forest" situated in the rolling pinelands of west-central Louisiana.

beautiful conservation area that covers 600,000 acres (242,820 hectares) in the central and northwestern part of the state.

Many Louisianians enjoy exploring the state's numerous and beautiful public gardens. The most famous is Hodges Gardens near Many, a breathtaking 4,700-acre (1,902-hectare) "garden in the forest." Other interesting gardens include Live Oak Gardens at Jefferson Island, Avery Island Jungle Gardens, Briarwood Gardens near Saline, Elsong Gardens in Monroe, Acadian Village and Garden near Baton Rouge, and Swamp Gardens in Morgan City. The Louisiana Purchase Gardens and Zoo in Monroe has beautiful landscaped gardens, exhibits about the Louisiana Purchase Territory, and a zoo. Two other popular zoos are the Baton Rouge Zoo and the Audubon Zoological Garden in New Orleans.

Historic Sites and Landmarks:

Audubon State Commemorative Area, near St. Francisville, is the site of Oakley Plantation, where John James Audubon served as a tutor while observing, collecting, and painting many of the birds for his famous *Birds of America*.

Chalmette National Historical Park, near New Orleans, was the site of the 1815 Battle of New Orleans.

119

Fort Jesup State Commemorative Area, near Many, was established in 1822 by General (later President) Zachary Taylor, and was the site of the United States Army's southernmost outpost until the Mexican War.

Fort Pike State Commemorative Area, east of New Orleans, was a fort constructed after the War of 1812 to defend navigational channels leading into New Orleans.

French Quarter in New Orleans, a National Historic Landmark, is an eighty-five-block area of French and Spanish Colonial-style architecture. Royal Street is noted for its antique shops and art galleries, and Bourbon Street for its restaurants, jazz clubs, and nightclub shows. Jackson Square is the site of two famous landmarks: St. Louis Cathedral, and a statue of Andrew Jackson on his horse.

Longfellow-Evangeline State Commemorative Area is a park on the banks of Bayou Teche near St. Martinville. Covered with live oaks, the beautiful 150-acre (60.7-hectare) park commemorates Longfellow's poem *Evangeline*.

Marksville State Commemorative Area, near Marksville, contains archaeological evidence of an Indian village and ceremonial center that flourished some two thousand years ago.

Natchitoches, founded in 1714, is the oldest continuously occupied settlement in Louisiana. The National Historic District in the heart of town features brick streets and balconies with wrought-iron railings. Fort St. Jean Baptiste de Natchitoches, the strategic outpost built to prevent the Spaniards in Texas from advancing into French Louisiana, has been reconstructed and is open to the public.

Oak Alley Plantation, between St. James and Vacherie on the Mississippi River, is a National Historic Landmark. Completed in 1839, it features an avenue of 300-year-old live oaks that leads all the way from the River Road to the mansion.

Old State Capitol, in Baton Rouge, was built in 1849. A blend of Norman, Gothic, and Moorish styles, it gives the appearance of a medieval castle.

Port Hudson State Commemorative Area, near Zachary, is the site of the Civil War's longest battle. Here, sixty-eight hundred Confederates under the command of Major General Franklin Gardner held out for forty-eight days against a Union army of thirty thousand.

Poverty Point State Commemorative Area, near Epps, is the site of the earliest Indian culture yet discovered in the Mississippi Valley, and is considered one of the most significant archaeological finds in the nation.

Other Interesting Places to Visit:

American Rose Center, near Shreveport, is the headquarters of the American Rose Society, the country's largest plant society. It features 118 acres (48 hectares) of spectacular rose gardens.

Shadows-on-the-Teche Plantation House, built in 1834 on the banks of the Bayou Teche, is a beautifully restored Greek Revival mansion.

Fort Humbug, in Shreveport, got its name during the Civil War, when Confederate soldiers disguised charred logs as cannon to "humbug" union scouts. Today it is a children's recreation area. Wooden cannon are still on display.

Houmas House Plantation, in Burnside, is a Greek Revival mansion that was completed in 1840. It is furnished with period antiques.

Louisiana State Arboretum, near Ville Platte, occupies 600 acres (243 hectares) of Chicot State Park. It features nature trails through plant life native to Louisiana.

Moss-Pitot House, in New Orleans, is a former plantation that has been restored in the style of the early 1800s and filled with Federal-period antiques.

Nottoway Plantation House, near Baton Rouge, is the South's largest plantation home.

Rosedown Plantation and Gardens, in St. Francisville, is a beautiful antebellum mansion that has been lavishly restored.

San Francisco Plantation House, in Reserve, is a restored mansion of the "Steamboat Gothic" style.

Shadows-on-the-Teche Plantation House in New Iberia, a Greek Revival mansion built in 1834, is one of the state's most authentically restored homes of its period.

State Capitol in Baton Rouge, Louisiana's current seat of government, is the nation's tallest state capitol.

IMPORTANT DATES

1700-700 B.C.—Inhabitants of Poverty Point in northeastern Louisiana, noted as builders of elaborate mounds, establish an advanced civilization

A.D. 100-550—The "Marksville Culture," a southeastern variant of the Hopewell Culture of Ohio and Illinois, flourishes

1500s—At time of first European exploration, some thirty different Indian groups live in what is now Louisiana, including the Tunica, Chitimacha, Attakapa, Caddo, Tensas, Houma, and various Muskhogean groups

1541—Spanish explorer Hernando De Soto discovers the Mississippi River

1682—French adventurer Sieur de La Salle follows the Mississippi River from the Great Lakes to the Gulf of Mexico; he erects a cross and column at the mouth of the river and claims the territory for France, naming it Louisiana in honor of his king, Louis XIV; the area he claimed encompassed the central third of the present-day United States

1699—French explorer Pierre Le Moyne, Sieur d' Iberville, founds the French colony of Louisiana and establishes a settlement at Biloxi Bay

1712—The king of France grants exclusive trading rights in Louisiana to Antoine Crozat, a French merchant

1714—Natchitoches, first permanent European settlement in what will become the state of Louisiana, is founded

1717—John Law's Company of the West receives exclusive charter for control and colonization of Louisiana

1718—Jean Baptiste Le Moyne, Sieur de Bienville, founds New Orleans

1719—John Law recruits 250 German farmers to the colony

1720—John Law's plan to finance colonization of Louisiana finally fails due to the collapse of his bank in France, but the Company of the Indies (previously the Company of the West) continues to control Louisiana

1722—New Orleans becomes the capital of the Louisiana colony; a disastrous hurricane destroys most of the city

1731—The failed Company of the Indies gives up its charter and Louisiana reverts to being a crown colony under Louis XV

1762—By the secret Treaty of Fountainbleau, France cedes to Spain all of the Louisiana colony west of the Mississippi River and the Isle of Orleans (New Orleans) on the river's east bank

1763—Treaty of Paris, ending the Seven Years' War in Europe, officially confirms the transfer of Louisiana to Spain

1764—Acadian families begin arriving in Louisiana

1766—Antonio de Ulloa becomes the first Spanish governor of Louisiana

1768—New Orleans settlers force out Spanish Governor Ulloa

1769—General Alejandro O'Reilly reinstates Spanish authority

1788—New Orleans is almost completely destroyed by fire; leaders of the city promptly rebuild

1794—A second great fire ravages New Orleans

1795—Twenty-five slaves are killed in the "Black Rebellion," a slave uprising in Pointe Coupee Parish; in New Orleans, Jean Etienne de Boré develops the first successful method of granulating sugar on a large scale

1800—By the Treaty of San Ildefonso, Spain secretly cedes Louisiana back to France

1803—The United States purchases Louisiana from France for about $15 million, thereby doubling the size of the United States

1804—Congress subdivides the vast Louisiana Territory into two parts: the District of Louisiana (which included all of present-day Montana, Nebraska, Iowa, Kansas, Missouri, Oklahoma, and Arkansas, and parts of North Dakota, South Dakota, Texas, Wyoming, Minnesota, Colorado, and New Mexico), and the Territory of Orleans (which covered about the same area as present-day Louisiana)

1811—Massive slave rebellion in St. John the Baptist Parish suppressed

1812—Louisiana admitted to the Union as the eighteenth state; first state constitution adopted; the golden era of the steamboat begins as the *New Orleans* arrives in New Orleans from Pittsburgh

1815—General Andrew Jackson defeats British General Pakenham and his troops at the Battle of New Orleans

1819—The United States and Spain sign a treaty whereby Spain concedes the west bank of the Sabine River as Louisiana's western boundary

1833—Captain Henry Miller Shreve begins clearing the Great Red River Raft, opening up northwestern Louisiana to settlement

1837—Shreveport founded

1845—A more democratic "Jacksonian" state constitution is adopted

1849—Baton Rouge replaces New Orleans as capital of Louisiana

1852—A new, more conservative, state constitution is adopted

1853—The worst yellow-fever epidemic in the history of the state kills eleven thousand people in New Orleans alone, and wipes out many small towns

1861—Louisiana secedes from the Union and joins the Confederacy

1862 — New Orleans is captured by Union forces under Captain David G. Farragut; General Benjamin F. Butler begins military rule in New Orleans; salt mine at Avery Island, the oldest commercial mine in the nation, is discovered

1863 — Confederate stronghold of Port Hudson falls to Union forces

1865 — The last Confederate forces in the field surrender; Louisiana comes under complete federal control, with seat of government at New Orleans

1868 — Louisiana is readmitted to the Union

1874 — The White League defeats the New Orleans government militia in the "Battle of Liberty Place," one of many acts of violence occurring throughout the state at this time

1877 — Federal troops are withdrawn from Louisiana; conservative Democrats regain control of the state government

1879 — A new state constitution is adopted; Baton Rouge is reinstated as the permanent state capital; the mouth of the Mississippi River is deepened, enabling oceangoing ships to reach New Orleans

1884 — World's Fair is held in New Orleans

1893 — A hurricane in southern Louisiana and Mississippi kills more than two thousand people

1896 — U.S. Supreme Court rules in *Plessy v. Ferguson* that the Louisiana law requiring "separate but equal" railroad cars for blacks and whites is constitutional; the landmark decision permitted racial segregation in other public facilities, notably public schools; attempt by the Populists to oust the Bourbons is defeated

1898 — State constitution is revised to include a "grandfather clause" allowing some illiterate whites to bypass the literacy requirement for voting that had been enacted to disqualify blacks

1901 — Oil is discovered for the first time in Louisiana, near Jennings

1909 — Louisiana's first oil refinery opens in Baton Rouge; sulfur mining begins in Calcasieu Parish

1910 — Edward Douglass White of Lafourche Parish is appointed chief justice of the United States Supreme Court

1916 — First commercial gas field in Louisiana is discovered near Monroe

1921 — A new state constitution, with amendments that bring it to a length of more than a thousand pages, is adopted

1927 — Louisiana suffers the worst flood in its history after a record winter rainfall causes the Mississippi River to overflow

1928 — Huey P. Long becomes governor

1929 — An attempt to impeach Governor Huey P. Long is defeated

1932 — Huey P. Long becomes a United States senator, but continues to control the state government

1935 — Huey P. Long is assassinated in Baton Rouge

1939 — Political scandals force resignation of Governor Richard W. Leche; Earl Long becomes governor

1947 — Louisiana's first offshore oil well is brought in south of Morgan City

1956 — The Lake Pontchartrain Causeway, the longest bridge in the world, is opened

1957 — Hurricane Audrey kills hundreds of people in Cameron Parish

1958 — New Orleans abolishes segregation on city buses

1960 — Two public schools in Orleans Parish are desegregated

1965 — Hurricane Betsy devastates southern Louisiana and kills at least sixty-one people

1973 — Lindy Boggs becomes Louisiana's first congresswoman after her husband, Congressman Hale Boggs, is killed in a plane crash

1975 — Eleventh state constitution goes into effect; Louisiana Superdome opened in New Orleans

1977 — New Orleans elects its first black mayor, Ernest N. "Dutch" Morial

1980 — David C. Treen becomes the first Republican Louisiana governor since Reconstruction

1984 — New Orleans hosts a world's fair, the 1984 Louisiana World Exposition

1987 — Cuban detainees at the Federal Detention Center in Oakdale seize the compound and hold twenty-six people hostage for eight days after it is announced that they will be sent back to Cuba

1989 — Former Ku Klux Klan grand wizard David Duke wins a seat in the state legislature; the legislature modernizes the Napoleonic Code with important new rules governing commercial transactions

JOHN JAMES AUDUBON

PIERRE BEAUREGARD

LINDY BOGGS

GEORGE W. CABLE

IMPORTANT PEOPLE

Antoine Alciatore (1813-1875), chef and restaurant owner; operated the famous New Orleans restaurant Antoine's, which glamorized the French-Creole tradition of food

Henry Watkins Allen (1820-1866), Confederate army brigadier general; governor of Confederate-controlled Louisiana (1863-65); helped keep Louisiana in the war by his efforts to secure and distribute manufactured goods, weapons, food, clothing, and medicine

Louis Daniel (Satchmo) Armstrong (1900-1971), born in New Orleans; jazz trumpeter, singer, composer, and entertainer; influenced jazz musicians around the world as a recording and performing artist; invented the "scat" singing style

John James Audubon (1785-1851), naturalist and painter; famous for his drawings of birds in their natural habitats; lived in the New Orleans and Bayou Sara regions while observing and drawing birds of the area for his famous *Birds of America*

Pierre Gustave Toutant Beauregard (1818-1893), born near New Orleans; Confederate brigadier general; directed the bombardment of Fort Sumter, which began the Civil War; commander at battles of Bull Run and Shiloh; director of the Louisiana state lottery, a major source of the state's revenue after the war

Sidney Bechet (1897?-1959), born in New Orleans; jazz musician; noted for his 1938 recording *Summertime*; one of the first jazz artists to gain recognition on the soprano saxophone

Judah Philip Benjamin (1811-1884), lawyer, Confederate statesman; published, with Thomas Slidell, Louisiana's earliest digest of state law; United States senator (1853-61); attorney general (1861), secretary of war (1861-62), and secretary of state (1862-65) of the Confederacy

Corinne Claiborne (Lindy) Boggs (1916-   ), born at Brunswick Plantation; first congresswoman from Louisiana (1973-1990)

Jean Etienne de Boré (1741-1820), born in Louisiana; planter; in 1795 helped found Louisiana's sugar industry by developing a commercial method for granulating sugar; first mayor of New Orleans (1803-04)

Terry Bradshaw (1948-   ), born in Shreveport; quarterback of the NFL Pittsburgh Steelers; led his team to four Superbowl titles during the 1970s

George Washington Cable (1844-1925), born in New Orleans; novelist, social reformer; noted for his colorful and sometimes critical portrayal of Creole life; early advocate of racial justice; most famous work was *Old Creole Days*

Truman Capote (1924-1984), born in New Orleans; novelist, short-story writer, playwright; noted for his prose style and colorful characterizations; famous works include his first novel, *Other Voices, Other Rooms*, and his "non-fiction novel" *In Cold Blood*

TRUMAN CAPOTE

Kate O'Flaherty Chopin (1851-1904), author; used her experiences of life on a Red River plantation and in New Orleans to portray Creole life; best known for her novels *Bayou Folk* and *The Awakening*

William Charles Coles Claiborne (1775-1817), politician; only governor of Territory of Orleans; first governor of the state of Louisiana (1812-16)

Henry Lavan (Van) Cliburn (1934-   ), born in Shreveport; internationally known concert pianist; first classical musician to receive a New York ticker-tape parade after he won first prize at Moscow's First International Tchaikovsky Piano Competition in 1958

VAN CLIBURN

James Houston (Jimmie) Davis (1902-   ), born in Jackson Parish; musician-composer, politician; governor of Louisiana (1944-48, 1960-64); during his first gubernatorial campaign, ran on a "peace and harmony" platform and traveled the state singing his composition "You Are My Sunshine"; became governor again in 1960 by running on a segregationist platform

Michael E. DeBakey (1908-   ), born in Lake Charles; surgeon; pioneer in the treatment of heart disease; developed more than fifty instruments and devices used in heart surgery; devised first successful "assisting heart," a mechanical pump that helps do the work for a diseased heart

MICHAEL DEBAKEY

Antoine (Fats) Domino, Jr. (1928-   ), born in New Orleans; pianist, bandleader; combined elements of blues and rock in the early years of rock and roll

James Eads (1820-1887), engineer; opened the Mississippi River to large ships by building jetties which scoured out the "mud lumps" that had obstructed navigation

Edwin W. Edwards (1927-   ), born in Avoyelles Parish; politician; governor of Louisiana (1972-80, 1984-88); as governor, helped bring in a new state constitution, promoted the construction of the Superdome sports arena, and increased state spending for education, state parks, and tourism; first person in Louisiana history to win a third term as governor

EDWIN EDWARDS

Peter Dewey (Pete) Fountain (1930-   ), born in New Orleans; Dixieland jazz clarinetist; first gained fame with the Lawrence Welk Orchestra; leading figure in New Orleans jazz scene

Bernardo de Gálvez (1746-1786), governor of Spanish Louisiana (1777); during last years of the American Revolution gave arms and provisions to the patriots, seized British ships, and took Baton Rouge and British-held Gulf coast

LOUIS GOTTSHALK

LILLIAN HELLMAN

MAHALIA JACKSON

JEAN BAPTISTE LE MOYNE

Louis Moreau Gottshalk (1829-1869), born in New Orleans; first internationally known American pianist and composer; his compositions were inspired by ethnic music, particularly Creole and black folk music

Shirley Ann Grau (1929-   ), born in New Orleans; author of novels and short stories about the South; received 1964 Pulitzer Prize in fiction for *The Keepers of the House*

Lafcadio Hearn (1850-1904), author, journalist; wrote for the *New Orleans Item* and *Times-Democrat*, wrote a number of works using Louisiana as a setting, including *Chita*, about the destructive tidal wave that swept Last Island in 1856

Lillian Hellman (1905-1984), born in New Orleans; playwright, screenwriter; attacked injustice, selfishness, and evil in such plays as *The Children's Hour, The Little Foxes*, and *Toys in the Attic*

Alois Maxwell (Al) Hirt (1922-   ), born in New Orleans; trumpeter, bandleader; soloist and stylist of jazz and popular music; first major recording was *The Greatest Horn in the World*

Mahalia Jackson (1911-1972), born in New Orleans; world-famous contralto known for her moving and vibrant interpretations of gospel music; helped to popularize gospel music

Grace Elizabeth King (1859-1932), born in New Orleans; novelist, historian; works deal with Louisiana and Creole themes

Jean Laffite (1780?-1826), French pirate; led a band of renegades whose headquarters were on the Islands of Barataria Bay south of New Orleans; plundered Spanish and neutral ships and then sold the booty illegally; for years eluded capture by the American government; when the British asked him to help them attack New Orleans during the War of 1812, he revealed their intentions to the American government; he and his men then volunteered to help Andrew Jackson defeat the British in the Battle of New Orleans; for his help in the battle, he and his men were pardoned for all past crimes; returned to piracy after the war

René-Robert Cavelier, Sieur de La Salle (1643-1687), French explorer; led first European expedition tracing the Mississippi River to the Gulf of Mexico; in 1682, claimed for France all the lands drained by the river and named the region Louisiana

John A. Law (1671-1729), Scottish financier; secured a trade monopoly from the king of France for all of the Louisiana territory; in 1717 formed the Company of the West to finance his plan for exploiting the region; in 1720, when his company collapsed due to overissuing of stock, he fled France in disgrace

Jean Baptiste Le Moyne, Sieur de Bienville (1680-1768), French-Canadian explorer; helped settle the French colony of Louisiana; explored lower Mississippi River area with his brother Pierre; governor of the French colony of Louisiana (1706-13, 1717-23, 1733-43); in 1718 founded New Orleans; served Louisiana longer than any other colonial official

Pierre Le Moyne, Sieur d'Iberville (1661-1706), explorer and military officer; in 1699 founded the French colony of Louisiana; led three expeditions to explore the lower Mississippi Valley; established Fort Maurepas (near present-day Biloxi, Mississippi), the first permanent settlement of the Louisiana colony

Earl Kemp Long (1895-1960), born near Winnfield; politician; brother of Huey Long; governor of Louisiana (1939-40, 1948-52, 1956-60); as governor, spoke out for racial reform, improvements in state education and social welfare benefits, and the enlargement of a statewide charity hospital system; this ensured his popularity with poor and black voters, but resulted in a heavy increase in state taxation

EARL LONG

Huey Pierce "the Kingfish" Long (1893-1935), born near Winnfield; lawyer, politician; most powerful political leader in Louisiana history; known as a champion of the poor; gained popularity through his support of social reforms; governor of Louisiana (1928-31); as governor, implemented a "progressive" social-welfare and public-works program whereby he improved highways, provided free textbooks, expanded the state's educational system, established a state hospital to provide free medical care, and increased taxes for the rich; established a powerful political machine and became virtually a dictator of Louisiana by appointing or supporting the elections of friends to state offices; in 1929 was charged with bribery and misappropriation of state funds but was never tried; took control of the state's legislature, courts, and municipal governments and attempted to control the news with his own newspaper; United States senator (1932-35); in 1935 was killed by the son-in-law of a political opponent

HUEY LONG

Russell Billiu Long (1918-   ), born in Shreveport; politician; son of Huey Long; United States senator (1948-86); became one of the most powerful men in Congress as chairman of the Finance Committee, (1965-81); favored simplified tax returns and heavier tax burden on the rich

RUSSELL LONG

John McDonough (1779-1850), businessman, philanthropist; offered the slaves on his plantation a chance to buy their freedom; his will left about $2 million to be divided between New Orleans and Baltimore for public schools

Ernest Nathan (Dutch) Morial (1929-1989), lawyer, jurist, politician; in 1968 became the first black person elected to the Louisiana legislature since Reconstruction; juvenile court judge in New Orleans (1970-72); Federal Appeals Court judge (1974-77); first black mayor of New Orleans (1978-86)

Jelly Roll Morton (1885-1941), born Ferdinand Joseph La Menthe in New Orleans; jazz musician, composer; in the 1920s made some of the earliest recorded examples of disciplined jazz-ensemble work

DUTCH MORIAL

MEL OTT

LEONIDAS POLK

ANDREW SCHALLY

HENRY SHREVE

Josephine Louise Newcomb (1816-1901), businesswoman, philanthropist; donated $100,000 for the creation of a women's college at Tulane University to be called the H. Sophie Newcomb Memorial College in honor of her daughter

Francis Tillou Nicholls (1831-1912), born in Donaldsonville; Confederate general; first governor after "carpetbag" rule ended (1877-80); governor (1888-92); chief justice of the state supreme court (1892-1911)

Alejandro O'Reilly (1725-1749), military officer and administrator; charged with the task of establishing Spanish rule in French Louisiana after the first Spanish governor, Antonio de Ulloa, was forced out; punished the leaders of the "rebels" who had opposed Ulloa and granted amnesty to all other colonists

Melvin Thomas (Mel) Ott (1909-1958), born in Gretna; baseball player and manager of the National League's New York Giants; first National League player to hit four hundred home runs; in 1951 elected to the National Baseball Hall of Fame

Walker Percy (1916-1990), novelist; resided in Covington; works include *The Moviegoer* and *The Second Coming*

Leonidas K. Polk (1806-1864), Episcopal bishop, educator, Confederate army lieutenant general; in 1841 became Louisiana's first Episcopal bishop; killed in fighting near Atlanta

Paul Prudhomme (1939-   ), internationally known chef; grew up south of Opelousas in Acadian country; in 1979 opened K-Paul's Louisiana Kitchen in New Orleans, a restaurant known for superb Cajun dishes; has led the way in spreading the popularity of Creole and Cajun food nationwide

Henry Hobson Richardson (1838-1886), born in St. James Parish; architect; help establish a truly "American" style of architecture; built the Howard Library in New Orleans

Bill Russell (1934-   ), born in Monroe; professional basketball player, coach, and general manager; as a player led the Boston Celtics to eleven NBA championships; was voted the league's Most Valuable Player five times; became the first black coach of a major professional sports team; in 1974 elected to the Basketball Hall of Fame

Andrew Victor Schally (1926-   ), biochemist on the faculty of Tulane University School of Medicine; shared the 1977 Nobel Prize in medicine for his research on hormones

Henry Miller Shreve (1785-1851), pioneer steamboat builder; contributed greatly to the development of the Mississippi waterway system; in the 1830s opened northern Louisiana to development by clearing the Red River of a massive logjam known as the "Red River Raft"; the workcamp he founded eventually became the city of Shreveport

John Slidell (1793-1871), lawyer, politician, diplomat; United States representative from Louisiana (1843-45); United States senator (1853-61); aligned himself with the Confederacy when Louisiana seceded from the Union; was sent to France to obtain French recognition of the Confederacy; an international incident known as the Trent Affair was created when Union forces captured him aboard a British vessel on the way to France; freed due to British pressure, he arrived in France, but was unsuccessful in negotiating with the French government

JOHN SLIDELL

Ruth McEnery Stuart (1849-1917), born in Avoyelles Parish; writer; told tales of southern life in such works as *A Golden Wedding and Other Tales* and *The Second Wooing of Salina Sue*

Richard Taylor (1826-1879), born in St. Charles Parish; Confederate military leader; son of Zachary Taylor; Louisiana state senator (1845-61); at beginning of the Civil War commanded a Louisiana infantry regiment; in 1862 promoted to major general and for next two years commanded district of West Louisiana; noted for defeat of General Bank's Union forces during the Red River campaign of 1864; in 1865 surrendered the last Confederate army east of the Mississippi

RICHARD TAYLOR

Zachary Taylor (1784-1850), twelfth president of the United States; United States Army brigadier general; commanded troops in the War of 1812, the Black Hawk War, and the Second Seminole War in Florida; established his home in Baton Rouge when assigned to a post in Louisiana in 1840; his brilliant performance as a commander during the Mexican War made him a national hero; was elected to the presidency (1849-50) on the basis of his distinguished military career, but died after only sixteen months in office

ZACHARY TAYLOR

Paul Tulane (1801-1887), New Orleans merchant; from 1882 on gave generously to the University of Louisiana, which in 1884 was renamed Tulane University in his honor

Antonio de Ulloa (1716-1795), Spanish scholar, naval officer, administrator; became the first Spanish governor of Louisiana (1766-68), but never assumed full powers; was ousted by rebellious Louisiana settlers who resented France ceding the territory to Spain

Henry Clay Warmoth (1842-1932), Union soldier, politician; Louisiana's first elected Republican governor (1868-72); later started sugar plantation near New Orleans and built the New Orleans, Fort Jackson, and Grand Isle railroads

Robert Penn Warren (1905-1989), novelist, poet; received 1947 Pulitzer Prize in fiction for *All the King's Men*, a fictionalized account of Huey Long's career; taught at Louisiana State University at Baton Rouge (1934-42); founded and edited the *Southern Review*

ROBERT PENN WARREN

EDWARD D. WHITE

Edward Douglass White (1845-1921), born in Lafourche Parish; lawyer and jurist; served in the state senate and the state supreme court in the 1870s; associate justice (1894-1910) and chief justice (1910-21) of the United States Supreme Court

T. Harry Williams (1909-1979), historian, teacher; received 1970 Pulitzer Prize in biography for his book *Huey Long*; taught history at Louisiana State University

GOVERNORS

W.C.C. Claiborne	1812-1816	Francis T. Nicholls	1877-1880
Jacques Philippe Villeré	1816-1820	Louis A. Wiltz	1880-1881
Thomas B. Robertson	1820-1824	Samuel D. McEnery	1881-1888
Henry S. Thibodaux	1824	Francis T. Nicholls	1888-1892
Henry Johnson	1824-1828	Murphy J. Foster	1892-1900
Pierre Derbigny	1828-1829	William W. Heard	1900-1904
Armand Beauvais	1829-1830	Newton C. Blanchard	1904-1908
Jacques Dupré	1830-1831	Jared Y. Sanders	1908-1912
André B. Roman	1831-1835	Luther E. Hall	1912-1916
Edward D. White	1835-1839	Ruffin G. Pleasant	1916-1920
André B. Roman	1839-1843	John M. Parker	1920-1924
Alexandre Mouton	1843-1846	Henry L. Fuqua	1924-1926
Isaac Johnson	1846-1850	Oramel H. Simpson	1926-1928
Joseph Walker	1850-1853	Huey P. Long	1928-1932
Paul O. Hebert	1853-1856	Alvin O. King	1932
Robert C. Wickliffe	1856-1860	Oscar K. Allen	1932-1936
Thomas O. Moore	1860-1864	James A. Noe	1936
George F. Shepley	1862-1864	Richard W. Leche	1936-1939
(military governor within Union lines)		Earl K. Long	1939-1940
		Sam H. Jones	1940-1944
Michael Hahn	1864-1865	Jimmie H. Davis	1944-1948
(elected governor within Union lines, resigned)		Earl K. Long	1948-1952
		Robert F. Kennon	1952-1956
Henry Watkins Allen	1864-1865	Earl K. Long	1956-1960
(elected governor within Confederate lines)		Jimmie H. Davis	1960-1964
		John J. McKeithen	1964-1972
James M. Wells	1865-1867	Edwin W. Edwards	1972-1980
Benjamin F. Flanders	1867-1868	David C. Treen	1980-1984
Joshua Baker	1868	Edwin W. Edwards	1984-1988
Henry C. Warmoth	1868-1872	Buddy Roemer	1988-
P. B. S. Pinchback	1872-1873		
William P. Kellogg	1873-1877		

MAP KEY

Place	Grid		Place	Grid		Place	Grid
Abbeville	D4		Calcasieu River (river)	D,E3		Port Barre	D4
Abita Springs	E6		Calcasieu Lake (lake)	D5,h11		Port Sulphur	E6
Addis	D5,h11		Calvin	C3		Port Vincent	D5,h10
Alexandria	C2		Cameron	D4		Powhatan	C2
Amelia	E6		Campti	C3		Provencal	C2
Amite	E6		Cane River (river)	E4,k9		Provencetown	E6
Amite River (river)	E6		Carencro	D5		Quitman	B3
Angie	B3		Carville	D,E,4,5,g,10		Raccourci Island (island)	D4
Arabi	k11		Castor	k11		Raceland	E5,k10
Arcadia	D6		Catahoula Lake (lake)	D6		Rayne	B4
Arnaudville	D4		Chalmette	k11		Rayville	D3
Ashland	D4		Chalmette National Historic Park	D4		Red River (river)	D2
Atchafalaya River (river)	B2		Chandeleur Islands (islands)	B2		Reeves	B4
Athens	B2		Chandeleur Sound (sound)	B2		Reserve	A,B,C,1,2
Atlanta	C3		Chataignier	D4		Ringgold	h10
Baker	E4		Chatham	C3		River Aux Chenes (river)	B2
Baldwin	B2		Chauvin	B2		River Ridge	k2
Ball	C3		Cheneyville	B2		Robeline	k11
Barataria	E4		Chicot Island (island)	C3		Rodessa	C2
Barataria Bay	B2		Choudrant	E4		Romeville	B1
Basile	E5,6		Church Point	B4		Roseland	h10
Baskin	E5,k10		Clarence	E5,k11		Rosepine	D5
Bastrop	k9		Clarks	E5,6		Ruston	D4
Baton Rouge	B3		Clayton	k9		Sabine River (river)	C2
Bayou Anacoco (bayou)	C4		Clinton	B3		Sabine Lake (lake)	B3
Bayou Black (bayou)	B3		Cloutierville	E5,k10		Saint Francisville	D4
Bayou Blue	E5,k10		Colfax	B4		Saint Joseph	C2
Bayou Bodcau Reservoir (reservoir)	B4		Collinston	E5,k10		Saint Martinville	D4,g9
Bayou Chene (bayou)	h9,10		Columbia	B4		Saline	B2
Bayou D'Arbonne (lake)	B2		Comite River (river)	h9,10		Saline Lake (lake)	h9
Bayou De Loutre (bayou)	D4		Converse	B2		Scott	B2
Bayou Dorcheat (bayou)	k10		Cottonport	D4		Scotlandville	B2
Bayou Lafourche (bayou)	B2		Cotton Valley	k10		Seymourville	C4
Bayou Macon (bayou)	E5,k12		Coushatta	B2		Shongaloo	B3
Bayou Manchac (bayou)	E4,k9		Covington	E5,k12		Shreveport	C2
Bayou Penchant (bayou)	B3		Crossing Lake (lake)	E4,k9		Sibley	B3
Bayou Teche (bayou)	B3		Crowley	B3		Sicily Island	B2
Bayou Terrebonne	C4		Cullen	B3		Sikes	B2
Belcher	B,C,3,4		Cut Off	C4		Stanley	D6,h12
Belle Chasse	h10		De Ridder	B,C3,4		Sterlington	D5,h10
Benton	D5,6		Delcambre	h10		Stonewall	D5,h10
Bienville	D4,h10		Delhi	D2		Sulphur	A2
Berwick	B3		Delta	D5,6		Sun	D2
Big Creek (creek)	D2		Denham Springs	D4,h10		Sunset	D2
Black River (river)	B2		De Quincy	D5,6		Tallulah	B3
Blind River (river)	E5		Des Allemands	B3		Tangipahoa	C,D,E2
Boeuf (bayou)	E5		Destrehan	B3		Tangipahoa River (river)	D4
Boeuf River (river)	D4		Dodson	C2		Tensas River (river)	D4
Bogalusa	E6		Donaldsonville	B3		Thibodaux	C4
Bonita	B,C3		Downsville	B4		Ticklaw	B3
Bonnet Carre Floodway	E4		Doyline	C4		Ticklaw River (river)	C3
Bossier City	D4,h9		Driskill Mountain (mountain)	E4		Timbalier Bay	B2
Bourg	B3		Dry Prong	D4,h9		Triumph	C2
Breaux Bridge	D2		Dubach	B3		Trout	D4
Breton Island (island)	E5		Dubberly	D3		Tullos	D5
Broussard	B1,2		Dugdemona (bayou)	B4		Turkey Creek	B2
Brusly	E6		Duson	E5,k11		Vacherie	E5,k10
Bryceland	E5		Elizabeth	E5,k11		Varnado	h10
Bunkie			Elton	D4,h10		Vermilion River (river)	D6
Buras			Epps	B3		Vidalia	E3
Caddo Lake (lake)			Erath	B3		Vienna	B4
Caillou Lake (lake)			Eros	E5		Ville Platte	D3

Place	Grid		Place	Grid		Place	Grid
Estherwood	D3		Lake Pontchartrain (lake)	D5,6,h11,12		Vinton	D4
Eunice	D3		Lake Pontchartrain Causeway	h11		Violet	B2
Evergreen	B3		Lafourche (Lake Providence)	B4		Vivian	B3
Farmerville	B3		Lake Salvador (lake)	k11		West Monroe	D6
Fenton	D3		Lake Verret (lake)	E4,k9		West Pearl River (river)	B2
Ferriday	C4			h11		Wallace Lake (lake)	B2
Fisher	C2		Laplace			Washington	D3
Florien	C2		Larose	E5		Waterproof	D3
Folsom	D5		Lawtell	C3		Welsh	E4
Fordoche	D5		Lecompte	C3		Westlake	D6
Forest Hill	C3		Leesville	D4		Westwego	D3
Fort Polk	D4		Leonville	B3		White Castle	C3
Franklinton	E4		Lisbon	B3		White Lake (lake)	C3
Freemason Island (island)	B2		Little River (river)	C3		Wilson	B2
French Settlement	D5,h10		Little Lake (lake)	E5		Winnfield	B4
Galliano	D4		Livingston	E7		Winnsboro	D4,h9
Garyville	E5		Livonia	D5,g10		Wisner	D2
Georgetown	D5,h10		Lockport			Woodworth	E5
Gibsland	C3		Logansport	C1,2		Youngsville	k10
Gilbert	B2		Longstreet	B2		Zachary	D5,h11
Gilliam	B4		Loreauville	D4		Zwolle	D4,h9
Glenmora	C3		Luling	k11			
Golden Meadow	E5		Lutcher	D5,h11			
Goldonna	B3		Madisonville	D5,h11			
Gonzales	D5,h10		Mamou	D3			
Grambling	B3		Mandeville	D3			
Grand Cane	B2		Mangham	B4			
Grand Coleau	D4		Mansfield	B2			
Grand Isle (island)	E6,k12		Mansura	D4			
Grand Lake (lake)	D2,3		Many	E4			
Grand Terre Island (island)	E6		Maringouin	E4			
Grassy Lake (lake)	k9		Marion	E6			
Grayson	B3		Marksville	B2			
Greensburg	D5		Marrero	k9			
Greenwood	B2		Marsh Island (island)	B3			
Gretna	E5,k11		Martin	D5			
Grosse Tete	B2		Maurice	B2			
Gueydan	C3		McNary	C3			
Gulf of Mexico			Melville	D4			
Hahnville	E6,k11		Mer Rouge	B4			
Hall Summit			Mermentau	E2			
Hammond	D5,h11		Mermentau River (river)				
Harahan	E7		Merryville	k11			
Harrisonburg	E6		Metairie	k11			
Harvey	D3		Minden				
Haughton	E5		Mississippi River (river)	C4			
Haynesville	E6		Mississippi Delta (delta)	A,B,C,D,E,4,5,6,g,9,h9,10,11;k11,12			
Heflin	E6		Monroe	E6			
Henderson	C3		Montgomery	B2			
Hessmer	C3		Montpelier	B2			
Hodge	C2		Mooringsport	C3			
Homer	B3		Moreauville	C3			
Hornbeck	C4		Morgan City	B3			
Hosston	C3		Morganza	C2			
Houma	C3		Morse	D4			
Ida	A2		Moss Bluff	D2			
Independence	D5		Mound	D5			
Intracoastal Waterway	B4		Napoleonville	E4,k9			
Iota	D4		Natchitoches	C2			
Iowa	D3		New Iberia	D4			
Jackson	D2		New Orleans	E5,h11			
Jamestown	B2		New Roads	D4			
Jeanerette	B4		New Sarpy	k11			
Jefferson	k11		Newellton	B4			
Jena	C4		Newllano	C2			
Jennings	D3		Noble	C2			
Jonesboro	B3		Norco	D5,h11			
Jonesville	E5		Norwood	D4			
Junction City	E4		Oak Grove	B4			
Kaplan	E4		Oak Ridge	D3			
Keatchie	B5		Oakdale	D3			
Kenner	E5,k11		Oberlin	D3			
Kentwood	D5,h10		Oil City	B2			
Kilbourne	D2		Olla	C3			
Killian	E5,k11		Opelousas	D3			
Kinder	D3		Ouachita River (river)	A,B,C,3,4			
Labadieville	E5,k10		Paincourtville	k9			
Lac Des Allemands (lake)	E5,k10		Palmetto	D4			
Lacombe	D6,h12		Parks	E4			
Lafayette	D4,h10		Patterson	E4			
Lafitte	k11		Pearl River (river)	D6			
Lake Arthur	D3		Pierre Part	E5			
Lake Arthur (lake)	D3		Pine Prairie	C3			
Lake Barre (lake)	B,C3		Pineville	C3			
Lake Bistineau (lake)			Pioneer	B2			
Lake Borgne (lake)	E4		Plain Dealing				
Lake Charles	D2		Plaquemine	D4,h9			
Lake De Cade (lake)			Plaucheville	D2			
Lake Fields (lake)	B4		Pleasant Hill	E5			
Lake Maurepas (lake)			Pollock	k10			
Lake Petit (lake)	B3		Ponchatoula	D5,h10,11			
			Port Allen			D5,h11	

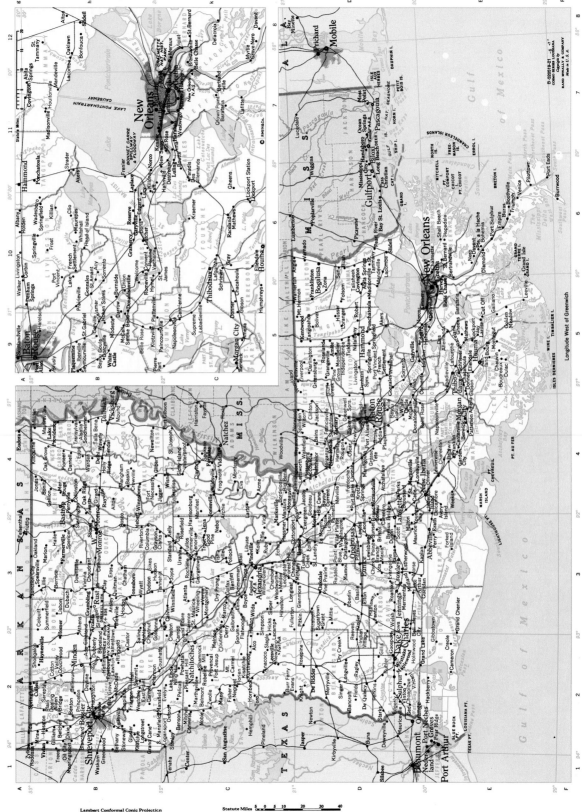

Lambert Conformal Conic Projection

Statute Miles

Kilometers

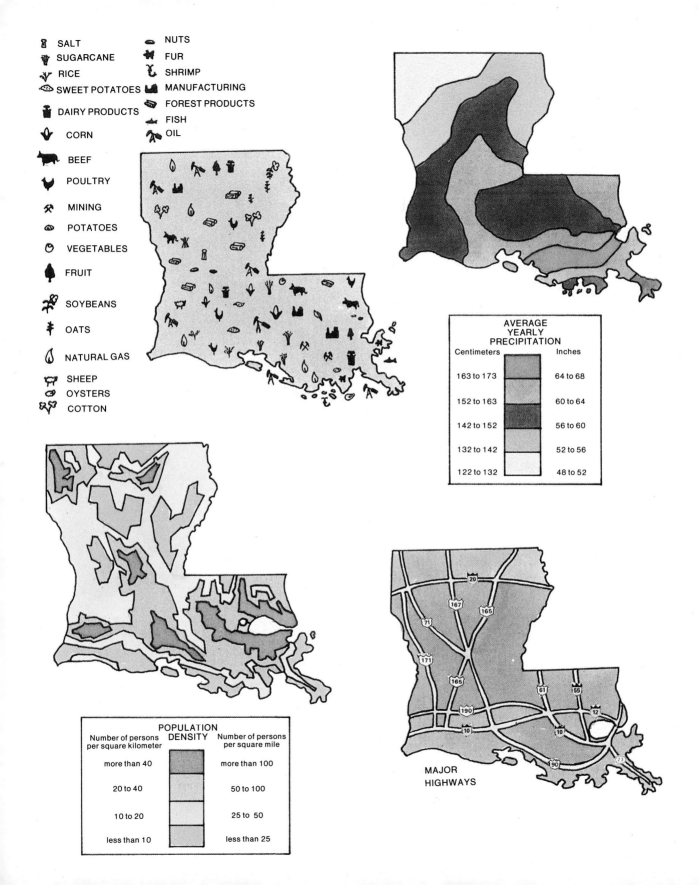

SALT

SUGARCANE

RICE

SWEET POTATOES

DAIRY PRODUCTS

CORN

BEEF

POULTRY

MINING

POTATOES

VEGETABLES

FRUIT

SOYBEANS

OATS

NATURAL GAS

SHEEP

OYSTERS

COTTON

NUTS

FUR

SHRIMP

MANUFACTURING

FOREST PRODUCTS

FISH

OIL

AVERAGE
YEARLY
PRECIPITATION

Centimeters		Inches
163 to 173		64 to 68
152 to 163		60 to 64
142 to 152		56 to 60
132 to 142		52 to 56
122 to 132		48 to 52

POPULATION
DENSITY

Number of persons per square kilometer		Number of persons per square mile
more than 40		more than 100
20 to 40		50 to 100
10 to 20		25 to 50
less than 10		less than 25

MAJOR
HIGHWAYS

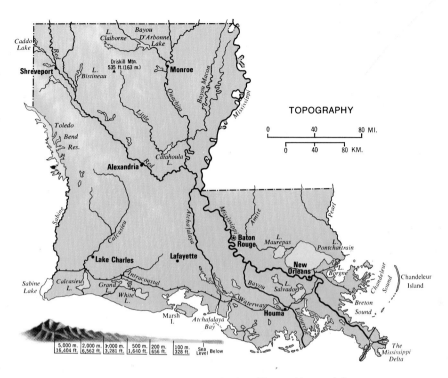

TOPOGRAPHY

0   40   80 MI.

0   40   80 KM.

Caddo Lake

Red

L. Claiborne

Bayou D'Arbonne Lake

Driskill Mtn. 535 ft. (163 m.)

Shreveport

L. Bistineau

Monroe

Ouachita

Bayou Macon

Mississippi

Little

Toledo Bend Res.

Catahoula L.

Red

Alexandria

Sabine

Calcasieu

Atchafalaya

Mississippi

Amite

Pearl

Baton Rouge

L. Maurepas

L. Pontchartrain

New Orleans

L. Borgne

Chandeleur Island

Chandeleur Sound

Sabine Lake

Calcasieu L.

Grand

White L.

Intracoastal

L. Salvador

Bayou

Waterway

Houma

Marsh I.

Atchafalaya Bay

Breton Sound

The Mississippi Delta

| 5,000 m. 16,404 ft. | 2,000 m. 6,562 ft. | 1,000 m. 3,281 ft. | 500 m. 1,640 ft. | 200 m. 656 ft. | 100 m. 328 ft. | Sea Level | Below |

Courtesy of Hammond, Incorporated
Maplewood, New Jersey

PARISHES

CADDO — Shreveport

BOSSIER — Benton

WEBSTER — Minden

CLAIBORNE — Homer

UNION — Farmerville

MOREHOUSE — Bastrop

WEST CARROLL — Oak Grove

EAST CARROLL — Lake Providence

LINCOLN — Ruston

OUACHITA — Monroe

RICHLAND — Rayville

MADISON — Tallulah

DE SOTO — Mansfield

RED RIVER — Coushatta

BIENVILLE — Arcadia

JACKSON — Jonesboro

WINN — Winnfield

CALDWELL — Columbia

FRANKLIN — Winnsboro

TENSAS — St Joseph

SABINE — Many

NATCHITOCHES — Natchitoches

GRANT — Colfax

LA SALLE — Jena

CATAHOULA — Harrisonburg

CONCORDIA — Vidalia

VERNON — Leesville

RAPIDES — Alexandria

AVOYELLES — Marksville

POINTE COUPEE — New Roads

WEST FELICIANA — St Francisville

EAST FELICIANA — Clinton

ST HELENA — Greensburg

TANGIPAHOA — Amite

WASHINGTON — Franklinton

BEAUREGARD — De Ridder

ALLEN — Oberlin

EVANGELINE — Ville Platte

ST LANDRY — Opelousas

WEST BATON ROUGE — Port Allen

EAST BATON ROUGE — Baton Rouge

LIVINGSTON — Livingston

ST TAMMANY — Covington

CALCASIEU — Lake Charles

JEFFERSON DAVIS — Jennings

ACADIA — Crowley

LAFAYETTE — Lafayette

ST MARTIN — St Martinville

IBERVILLE — Plaquemine

ASCENSION — Donaldsonville

ST JAMES — Convent

ST JOHN THE BAPTIST — Edgard

ST CHARLES — Hahnville

ORLEANS — New Orleans

ST BERNARD — Chalmette

CAMERON — Cameron

VERMILION — Abbeville

IBERIA — New Iberia

ST MARTIN — Franklin

ASSUMPTION — Napoleonville

LAFOURCHE — Thibodaux

JEFFERSON — Gretna

PLAQUEMINES — Pointe a la Hache

TERREBONNE — Houma

ST MARY

Louisiana State University at Baton Rouge is the state's largest university.

INDEX

Page numbers that appear in boldface type indicate illustrations

139

New Orleans' Garden District, in the city's Uptown area, is famous for its beautiful old mansions. Unlike the French Quarter, which was built by the early Spanish and French colonists, the Garden District was developed by Americans who came to New Orleans after the Louisiana Purchase in 1803.

A balcony in the French Quarter of New Orleans

Picture Identifications
Front cover: Spanish architecture in the French Quarter of New Orleans
Back cover: A Louisiana bayou
Pages 2-3: St. Louis Cathedral in New Orleans' Jackson Square
Page 6: A tourist stern-wheeler on the Mississippi River
Pages 8-9: A swamp in the Atchafalaya Basin
Pages 18-19: Montage of Louisiana residents
Page 28: La Salle claiming the Mississippi Valley region for France
Pages 38-39: A plantation on the Mississippi River in the 1800s
Pages 50-51: Union cavalry passing through Baton Rouge in 1863
Page 60: Southern sharecroppers picking berries in the early 1900s
Page 72: The State Capitol in Baton Rouge
Pages 80-81: A float in New Orleans' Mardi Gras Parade
Pages 92-93: The oak alley leading to Rosedown Plantation in St. Francisville
Page 92 (inset): Bourbon Street in the French Quarter of New Orleans
Page 108: Montage showing the state flag, the state flower (magnolia), the state tree (bald cypress), the state bird (brown pelican), and the state insect (honeybee)

Picture Acknowledgments

H. Armstrong Roberts: Page 118; ° M. Spector: Front cover; ° M. Burgess: Page 98 (left); ° H. Abernathy: Page 119
° **The Photo Source:** Pages 2-3
Root Resources: ° Garry D. McMichael: Pages 4, 6, 16, 19 (bottom right), 33 (left), 76 (right), 92-93, 99, 100, 113, 116; ° Art Brown: Page 12 (right); ° Earl L. Kubis: Page 15 (crawfish); ° Mike Dunn: Page 76 (left); ° James Blank: Pages 95, 106 (left), Back cover; ° Mary A. Root: Pages 108 (magnolia), 141; ° John Kohout: Page 108 (bee)
Photri: Pages 31, 38-39, 44, 53; ° J. McCauley: Pages 5, 19 (top right), 80-81; ° Leonard Lee Rue: Page 15 (nutria); ° Les Riess: Pages 18 (bottom left, bottom center), 24, 75, 86 (top left, bottom right), 89 (bottom right), 90 (bottom left), 105 (middle right)
Journalism Services: ° William H. Kildow: Pages 8-9; ° Don Allen, Donlen Inc.: Pages 12 (left), 79 (both photos), 98 (right); ° Jim Zietz: Pages 18 (top left), 19 (top left, bottom left), 25, 26, 86 (top right, bottom left), 138; ° Prather Warren: Pages 47 (top left), 72, 89 (top right); ° Larry Fields: Page 90 (top left)
Nawrocki Stock Photo: ° Robert Perron: Page 11; ° Wm. S. Nawrocki: Pages 18 (bottom right), 23 (left); ° Jeffrey Apoian: Page 86 (center); ° Steve Vidler: Page 105 (top right)
Cameramann International Ltd.: Pages 15 (Spanish moss), 18 (top right), 21, 45, 47 (top right, bottom), 48 (left), 89 (left), 92 (inset), 96 (left), 97, 103 (left), 105 (top left), 121
° **Lynn M. Stone:** Pages 15 (deer), 108 (pelican)
Tom Stack & Associates: ° Brian Parker: Pages 15 (alligator), 108 (tree); ° Rod Planck: Page 15 (heron)
Louisiana Office of Tourism: Pages 23 (right), 90 (top right, bottom right)
The Bettmann Archive: Pages 28, 33 (right), 37, 46, 55 (both photos), 60, 63, 67, 126 (Audubon, Beauregard, Cable), 127 (Cliburn), 128 (all photos), 130 (Polk, Shreve), 131 (Slidell, R. Taylor, Z. Taylor)
Historical Pictures Service, Inc., Chicago: Pages 34 (both photos), 35, 41, 50-51, 54, 56, 57, 59, 85, 129 (E. Long)
Roloc Color Slides: Pages 48 (right), 96 (right)
Jennings Carnegie Public Library: Page 64
Valan Photos: ° Harold V. Green: Pages 71, 105 (bottom right)
° **Arch McLean:** Page 101 (both photos)
Marilyn Gartman Agency: ° Rene Sheret: Page 103 (right), 105 (middle left, bottom left), 142
° **James P. Rowan:** Page 106 (right)
UPI/Bettmann: Pages 126 (Boggs), 127 (Capote, DeBakey), 129 (H. Long, R. Long)
Wide World Photos: Pages 127 (Edwards), 129 (Morial), 130 (Ott, Schally), 131 (Warren), 132
Len W. Meents: Maps on pages 95, 100, 103, 136
Courtesy Flag Research Center, Winchester, Massachusetts 01890: Flag on page 108

About the Author

Deborah Kent grew up in Little Falls, New Jersey, and received her B.A. in English from Oberlin College. She holds a Masters degree in Social Work from Smith College School for Social Work, and a Master of Fine Arts in Creative Writing from the University of Guanajuato in Mexico. Ms. Kent worked as a social worker in New York City and taught disabled children in Mexico before she began to write full-time.

Deborah Kent is the author of several novels for young adults, as well as this and other titles in the *America the Beautiful* series. She lives in Chicago with her husband and her daughter Janna.